CASE STUDIES IN

CULTURAL ANTHROPOLOGY

GENERAL EDITORS
George and Louise Spindler
STANFORD UNIVERSITY

THE AMERICAN CHILDREN OF KṚṢṆA

A Study of the Hare Kṛṣṇa Movement

THE AMERICAN CHILDREN
OF KṚṢṆA

A Study of the Hare Kṛṣṇa Movement

By

FRANCINE JEANNE DANER
University of Texas at Dallas

HOLT, RINEHART AND WINSTON
NEW YORK   CHICAGO   SAN FRANCISCO   ATLANTA
DALLAS   MONTREAL   TORONTO   LONDON   SYDNEY

Dedicated to my parents, Louis and
Ginger Daner, and to my friend Yvonne.

Photographs by Marjorie Daner-Sós

Library of Congress Cataloging in Publication Data

Daner, Francine Jeanne.
The American children of Kṛṣṇa.

(Case studies in cultural anthropology)
Bibliography: p. 116
1. Krishna—Cult. 2. International Society for
Krishna Consciousness. I. Title. II. Series.
BL1220.D35   301.5′8   75-15616
ISBN 0-03-013546-X

Portions of this book appeared in the author's doctoral
dissertation, copyright © 1974 by Francine Jeanne
Daner.

Foreword

ABOUT THE SERIES

These case studies in cultural anthropology are designed to bring students, in beginning and intermediate courses in the social sciences, insights into the richness and complexity of human life as it is lived in different ways and in different places. They are written by men and women who have lived in the societies they write about and who are professionally trained as observers and interpreters of human behavior. The authors are also teachers, and in writing their books they have kept the students who will read them foremost in their minds. It is our belief that when an understanding of ways of life very different from one's own is gained, abstractions and generalizations about social structure, cultural values, subsistence techniques, and the other universal categories of human social behavior become meaningful.

ABOUT THE AUTHOR

Francine Daner is a member of the American Anthropological Association, the Society for Medical Anthropology, and the Northeastern Anthropological Association. The original field research for the Hare Krsna study was done for her Ph.D. degree. In addition to publishing a number of articles about the Hare Krsnas and contemporary religion, the author frequently delivers public lectures on these subjects.

Her degrees include an M.A. in archaeology from Columbia University and a Ph.D. from the University of Illinios in 1973. Her interests are varied and extensive with special attention dedicated to medical and urban anthropology. Extensive field work in Latin America, both as an archaeologist and an ethnologist, led her to work in Oaxaca, Mexico, with an urban squatter's settlement and some native Zapotec curers.

Dr. Daner's interest in contemporary American ethnology arises from her fascination with the news media and her hobby of reading several newspapers daily. Her favorite papers range from the *New York Times*, to the *Boston Phoenix*, and to the obscure *New Journal*. She is presently working on a study of urban single-parent families.

ABOUT THE BOOK

This is a case study of the International Society for Krsna Consciousness (ISK-CON). For more than three years the author maintained close contact with the ISKCON community. During 1972 she worked intensively as a participant observer with the devotees in Boston, New York, London, and Amsterdam, with occasional visits to other temples. She still visits the Boston temple regularly and corresponds with people elsewhere in the movement. She was able to carry on an intimate participant observer study of the ISKCON community without interference or rejection for "Krsna Consciousness is an Open Secret." It is particularly appropriate in view of this attitude on the part of the devotees, including the officials of the community and its religious leaders, that Francine Daner should describe ISKCON with respect and sympathy as well as with the objectivity of anthropology.

There is much that could be commented on in a Foreword, but it seems unnecessary to anticipate what the author has written so carefully. The Children of Krsna are indeed the children of a philosophy and religious orientation that seems very remote from the center of American culture. Selfless devotion and loving service (bhakti) to Krsna involves behaviors, attitudes, and states of mind that many Americans may find not only esoteric but abhorrent. This is not because members of ISKCON take drugs, drink to excess, practice sexual libertarianism, commit crimes, or advocate radical political action. They do not. Rather, negative feelings are often aroused by a confrontation with values that strike at the core of American culture or at least appear to. If the Protestant Ethic and Calvinism are still alive in our culture, they may be seen as the counterpoint to ISKCON ideology and behavior. The Children of Krsna lose themselves in devotion to their deities, including a living representative of god in the form of Bhaktivedenta. They prostrate themselves before their religious leaders. They place negative value on education, on science, in knowledge of other than that to be gained through devotion. They deny the goodness of their own bodies and carnal passions. They are against war and violence. They beg on the streets and chant. And they have accepted a foreign religion, ideology, and philosophy from the East.

The esoteric qualities of ISKCON belief and behavior would lead one to assume that in every respect they represent a departure from American values. This may not be the case, for indeed asceticism, carnal denial, devotion to other-worldly qualities, and everlasting work in devotion to a cause are very much a part of an old American tradition leading back in time to the Puritans. Fundamentalism and asceticism with accouterments of various kinds have always been and will probably continue to be an integral part of the American scene.

At the same time, we must avoid trying to co-opt the Children of Krsna into the mainstream of American middle class Anglo culture. This is where most of them came from, and what appears to be a search for a startling alternative is also, of course, a deep rejection of contemporary social norms and cultural values. Francine Daner develops her analysis using alienation, search for identity, and revitalization as central concepts. She also sees recruitment as a vital process and discusses it in terms understandable to anthropologists, drawing from the works of Turner, Van Gennep, and others.

The reader will find this case study a good balance between solid ethnography, documentation from published sources, and analysis utilizing recognizable and appropriate anthropological theory.

GEORGE AND LOUISE SPINDLER
General Editors

Phlox, Wisconsin

Contents

Foreword   v

Acknowledgments   ix

Introduction   1

1. Hippies into Happies   6
   Manifestation of a Problem: Alienation   6
   The Underlying Problem: Identity   9
   A Possible Solution: The ISKCON Temple   12

2. A Guru Comes from India   15
   Krsna Comes to Second Avenue   17
   I Kiss Your Lotus Feet   17
   A Guru—The Direct Route to God   20

3. Roots in India   23
   Scripture: The Ideology   23
   The Guru Returns to India   30

4. The Concept of Bhakti: Its Meaning for Devotees   33
   The Temple   37
   The Daily Round   39
   Greeting the Lord: The Aratrika Ceremony   44
   Tulasi Devi Worship   47
   Jhulana-yatra: The Swing Ceremony   48
   The Calendrical Round   49

5. Transcendental Mechanics: The Practical Aspects of Temple Life   52
   Political Structure   52
   Conflict and Factionalism   55
   Economic Activities   56
   Socialization of Devotees   60
   Marriage   66
   Children and Education   68

6. I Am Not This Body   72
   The Devotees   77
   His Holiness Vasudeva dāsā Gosvāmī: A Biography   79

Yasoda devi dasi: A Biography   82
Diane: A Biography   86
Yvonne and Janardana dasa Adhikari: An Autobiography   88

7. Conclusions   102
      The Future of ISKCON   104

Appendixes   107

Glossary   113

References   116

Acknowledgments

I would like to thank the devotees without whose help this book could not have been written. I owe special thanks also to Bill Gardenier for his constant help and encouragement, to Dr. Gerhardt Duda, who listened, and to Nancy Lenicheck for her editorial assistance. I also benefited from the helpful comments of my friends Carol Stack, Eliot Singer, and John Kliphan. To "Yvonne" I feel the deepest friendship and respect for her courage in revealing to me the deepest and sometimes most painful parts of her life. I am also grateful for the criticisms and suggestions of my professors of the Department of Anthropology, Drs. Joseph Casagrande, Harold Gould, and Douglas Butterworth. Thanks are also due to the late Professor Oscar Lewis and to Ruth Lewis, who offered sympathetic guidance at many junctures in my career. And to Jayadvaita dāsa, my gratitude both for his kindness, and for his technical advice and assistance.

To Marjorie Daner-Sós who devoted so much time and effort taking the photographs for this book, I am much indebted.

F. J. D.

*. . . these orphans
of technocracy . . . weary and heavy-
laden, bow on bellies at Altar.
At last, after Vietnam, after Kent State,
after Watergate, a resting place at
many petalled Lotus Foot of Guru.*

—Richard Titlebaum

Introduction

The following work is an effort to present Krsna Consciousness as an aspect of what Toffler (1970:259) calls a "surfeit of subcults" that have arisen in American technocratic society. Contemporary American society has bred endless numbers of religious cults[1] and adopted foreign religions. One finds the pages of underground newspapers[2] crammed with news of such religions as Christianity, Zen, Buddhism, Sufism, Satanism, primitive shamanism, and Hinduism. Likewise, no anti-war demonstration or youth scene would be complete without a cowbelled contingent of holy men chanting the Hare Krsna mantra.

The yellow-robed men and women who chant this mantra are members of the International Society for Krsna Consciousness (ISKCON), whose chosen mission is to bring the Hindu (more correctly, Vedic) cult of Krsna worship to modern western society. Their goal is to change the polluted atmosphere until pure love of God (Krsna) dominates modern society. Each individual strives to cleanse his soul in order to obtain release from the endless wheel of birth and rebirth and to achieve liberation for his soul. The devotees of Krsna, as they call themselves, have organized into an elaborate network of temples (asramas) located throughout urban United States and in various other modern cities around the world.[3] Here they chant, dance, feast and seek converts to their ascetic Vedic religion.

An eclectic predilection for mystical, occult, magical phenomena has been characteristic of youth since the beatnik days of the 1950s. The interest in eastern religion can be viewed as an important aspect of youth's present interest in religion and spiritual matters, irrational and mystical thoughts as opposed to materialism, rationalism, and the almost religious acceptance of science espoused by their parents.

---

[1] Eister (1972:320), in an attempt to clarify the confusion between the concepts of sect and cult, uses the following definitions:

sect—"a group formed in protest against, and usually separating from, another religious group." (Warner 1964:624)

cult—"a loosely structured and often transitory and small voluntary association of people who share unique and generally world-denying religious values and/or who engage in bizarre religious rites." (Hoult 1969:90)

It is also important to note that ISKCON (International Society for Krsna Consciousness) members often refer to themselves as a cult.

[2] The underground press, a name used mostly for its romantic connotations, carries news and information on drugs, sexual liberation, rock music, Asian religions, anti-war and student struggles. The editorial line relentlessly blasts the "straight, authoritarian world," and supports all aspects of the struggle for "total freedom." Liberation of the spirit through karma forces, LSD, and music are familiar themes.

[3] See Appendix IV.

The history and literature extending out of nineteenth-century American tran-scendentalism (Emerson, Thoreau, Whitman, Hawthorne), together with the Theosophists, the Vedanta society, and so on, have long provided alternatives to the scientific world view and to the traditional churches of America. Yet these organiza-tions seem to have provided little direct influence on the current youth interest in eastern religions. Certainly it is nothing new that there should exist anti-rationalist elements in our midst; what is new, however, is that the radical rejection of science and technological values should appear so close to the center of society rather than on its margins. As Roszak (1969:51) observes, "It is the middle class young who are conducting this politics of consciousness, and they are doing it boisterously, persistently, and aggressively."

Factions of youth who choose to follow the exotic eastern religions do so because they feel that the prevailing scientific world view has left society devoid of a philosophy and language addressed to the nonintellectual, the irrational, and the mystical. The techniques and vocabularies of the Buddhist and Hindu traditions have been appropriated by youth for their explorations of mysticism precisely because they are antithetical to that conventional science held in such high esteem by the parent generation. In this way youth is striking a blow at the very founda-tions of technocratic society, seeking to undermine or even destroy many of its underlying assumptions. Thus a movement such as ISKCON is a reformist religious movement or what anthropologists have called a revitalization movement[4]; one which seeks the destruction of existing institutional forms and the construction of more satisfying forms.

ISKCON, with its highly structured organization, ideology, ancient ritual, and its clear-cut goal of changing society, can be considered a revitalization movement. However, the many revitalization studies done by anthropologists (Herskovits 1938; Wallace 1956; Barnett 1957; LaBarre 1962; Mooney 1965; Worsley 1968; Deloria 1971) have emphasized "the introduction of earlier religious or political forms" (Harris 1971:652) whereas ISKCON deliberately borrows an exotic religion and culture. Although the ISKCON philosophy is ancient in India, it is new and different to American society, a vehicle for the devotee's expression of disgust with society and with the values of the parent generation.

Revitalization studies have considerably enriched our knowledge of socio-religious movements; however, they have failed to concentrate upon the interaction between the psychological and sociological aspects of conversion as deeply as the theoretical work of Erikson (1950, 1956, 1958) and Goffman (1959, 1961). I feel Erikson's concepts of identity and alienation best explain why an individual chooses ISKCON over other alternatives open to him, while Goffman's concept of total institution and his symbolic interaction theories are useful in understanding the behavior of the ISKCON membership. Investigation of the apparently disori-ented life styles of ISKCON devotees prior to entrance into the temple confirmed my feeling that identity and alienation problems were key factors in the lives of the devotees. Constantly repeated themes were: "I did not know who I was," or "I was

---

[4] A revitalization movement is a "deliberate organized conscious effort by members of a society to seek a more satisfying culture" (Wallace 1956:265).

not self-realized." These demonstrated to me the usefulness of Erikson's work in organizing and interpreting my ethnographic observations. I have relied, therefore, on a great deal of biographical data to illustrate the value disorientation of individuals prior to their recruitment into ISKCON. It is the haphazardness of these life styles that the individuals seek to discard upon entrance into a temple where life is organized in every aspect.

I chose to study ISKCON because it is probably the largest and best organized[5] of the counter-culture religions, and one without the aura that exists in other alternative religious groups.[6] My curiosity about this religion was first aroused as I watched devotees chanting on the streets of Boston. A visit to the temple proved that ISKCON would be an important part of the contemporary scene for some time to come. I was amazed at the level of participation and the depth of sincerity which the ISKCON members exhibited, and I made an immediate decision to learn why young people were turning to this type of religion with such fervor. An investigation of the anthropological and sociological literature revealed the need for a study of counter-culture (or alternative) religions. Heretofore they had been dealt with by newspapers and magazines as bizarre curiosities, to be presented for their amusement value rather than their sociological importance. After my preliminary introduction to ISKCON, I was convinced that the time had come to introduce a serious study of an alternative religion into the wealth of tongue-in-cheek articles being produced by the popular press.

Religious movements of great dynamism such as peyote religion (Aberle 1966), the ghost dance (Mooney 1965), cargo cults (Worsley 1968), and other revitalization religions have often swept quickly over large populations, and these have been well treated by social scientists. The new religions, although widespread, have had little or no serious treatment. The most outstanding work is philosopher Jacob Needleman's *The New Religions* (1972) which, in addition to giving the history of some popular eastern religions in America, was written to describe the philosophical basis of each cult from the viewpoint of a potential practitioner. Although it is subjective, Needleman's work is a useful introduction to some of the religions which are currently capturing American youth.

Another welcome addition to the anthropological literature is *The Hippie Ghetto* by Partridge (1973), a work which regards hippie ghetto groups as "part of and a product of American society." This view is in direct disagreement with Roszak's *The Making of a Counter Culture* (1968), which categorizes all such subcultural groups under the heading of counter culture. Partridge (1973:67) joins Wallace (1969) in pointing out that the basic hippie values derive from our western cul-

---

[5] It is extremely difficult, if not impossible, to determine the size of ISKCON because the leaders themselves do not know precisely how many people belong. No membership records are kept; therefore the only way to get an accurate figure would be to conduct a census of all sixty-three ISKCON temples in the world, which, for this study, was totally impossible. Even temple presidents are confused about the exact number of members in their temple at any given time. No attendance is taken.

[6] The Process, another popular alternative religion, for example, is large and well organized, but the inquirer meets with much secrecy. There are special meetings and ceremonies for those who have advanced through the hierarchical ranks which are closed to all others, including Process members not of the prescribed rank. As an individual progresses through the ranks, new secrets are revealed to him at each level.

tural heritage and Judeo-Christian mythology. Partridge further notes that "most Americans subscribe to the validity of many points of the hippie ideology" because the central values are belief in individual salvation through good works, spiritual growth derived from meditation and prayer, and individual guilt and sin. These values, as we shall see in later chapters, are echoed in ISKCON culture; in fact, it seems that the devotees are trying to prove to the world that they can live their ideals rather than just mouth them. Most devotees describe themselves as having been hippies in the past, and it is to the hippie and the college student that their major proselytizing efforts are directed.

From March 1971 to June 1974 I maintained close and constant contacts with the ISKCON community. During the year 1972 I worked intensively as a participant observer with the devotees in Boston, New York, London, and Amsterdam, occasionally visiting other temples. I still visit the Boston temple regularly and correspond with some people from other temples irregularly. Most devotees like to receive letters and are sometimes willing to write letters in order to receive them. Their letters praise Krsna or give news of ISKCON's progress, and some personal news is usually included in the otherwise heavy handed missives.

At first I approached the temple president and some of the more established members of ISKCON in order to explain my intentions and request permission to do my research. Almost no one wanted to hear my explanation; most simply said that any good publicity for ISKCON was a service to Krsna and would be considered good karma for me. Besides, as they proclaimed, "Krsna Consciousness is an open secret! We have no personal life." Everyone agreed that I could do whatever I wanted, so I went ahead with my participant observation, joining into as many activities as my physical stamina would allow. There were times when I found chanting and dancing for long periods to be a great release for tension and anxiety in the same way an invigorating jog might be. During the course of my work, several members finally did become curious about it. Although they did not want to look at it themselves, they suggested that I show the finished piece to some higher ranking members for their official approval. Various chapters were read by some of the more interested devotees who volunteered their comments usually while remarking, "I should not be reading this; it is mental speculation." Other devotees never asked or cared what I was doing in the temple, and never turned off the preaching. The few constructive criticisms and comments given to me were incorporated into the work, and were, indeed, very helpful. I was sorry that I received so little feedback, as I had unrealistically expected more.

I met the same reluctance from the devotees to discuss their personal histories, so at first I put the subject aside. They would, however, often reminisce about their past lives during activities or casual conversations, and after a few months of my constant presence, I was accepted as a friend and ally. The devotees then began to relax in my presence and carry on normally, no longer regarding me as a guest. When I broached the subject again, virtually all discussed their life histories with me and were as cooperative as possible. In general, I found the devotees to be extremely sincere, kind, intelligent, and helpful young people, many of whom I now regard as friends.

For their protection, the real names of devotees are not used. The initiated members are designated by the use of such Indian names as they might be given at initiation; fictitious English names are used for uninitiated members and ex-members.

Much to my regret I was never able to get a personal interview with Bhakti-vedanta Swami, ISKCON's guru. Although I made several attempts I never succeeded in seeing him in private.

1 / Hippies into happies

I offer my humble obeisances unto His Divine Grace Prabhupada A. C. Bhaktivedanta Swami . . .
who supplanted the old-white bearded Judaic-Christian God with a beautiful,
blue adolescent boy and evoked gopi-tears from the eyes of men.
who listened, tolerant, to the threats of Jewish, Catholic and protestant mothers
accusing him of stealing their sons, and offered them bananas, apples, dates,
tangerines, and charmed them with his smile.
who declared that Colonel Sanders of the Fried Chickens of Kentucky would have
to undergo a chicken-birth-life and death for every chicken smeared with his
recipe making its saucy way into the all-devouring mouths of the American
Karmavores. (Hayagriva dasa Adhikari)

A. C. Bhaktivedanta Swami is only one of many Indian gurus and swamis
who have established a following in America. Bhaktivedanta Swami's followers,
robed in yellow and orange and yielding their begging bowls like citizens of Delhi
or Calcutta, dance and chant melodic mantras. The young men with shaven heads,
their bodies and faces painted with white clay stripes, remain for hours in "ecstasy"
on the streets of our major cities. These are the members of the International
Society for Krsna Consciousness (ISKCON), formed by Bhaktivedanta Swami and
held together by mutual agreement to accept the principles of "bhakti-yoga."

Who are these people and why are they doing these strange things? These are
questions to be explored in this work. In addition, we shall attempt to place them
in the contemporary youth scene, and to relate their existence to the phenomenon
of alienation which itself is only the manifestation of a deeper problem, that of
identity.

MANIFESTATION OF A PROBLEM: ALIENATION

During the mid-fifties, a small group of assorted writers, artists and their entourage gathered in and around San Francisco and New York and soon became known
as "beatniks." Distinctive elements of their life style were a glorification of poverty,
a predilection for music and jargon, an interest in Eastern mysticism and French
existentialism, political apathy, and a general antagonism toward American society.

Press coverage quickly gave "beats" a notoriety that belied their small numbers.
Hallucinogenic drugs coupled with idolatry of Timothy Leary and Allen Ginsberg
spread from the small group to claim a large following on college campuses in the

1960s: the hippies. Concurrently, the silence of youth during the 1950s was broken and replaced by political action. Although the civil rights and black power movements of the 1960s had important components outside the campus scene, they were over-shadowed and for a large part embraced by new-left groups on college campuses. To an even larger extent, this also held true for anti-Vietnam war activity. Finally, political action geared toward redefining the role of the university within society at large and toward changing the distribution of power and authority within the university, was more directly confined to the campus proper.

During the second part of the 1960s, opposition among youths became more pervasive including larger numbers of college students. At this same time the hippie cult grew into what has been called the "counter culture" (Roszak 1969; Keniston 1971). The groups comprising the new counter culture drew their membership mostly from the educated, privileged children of the American dream, who found their society flawed and failing. Counter-culture philosophy seemed to represent a break from society's prescribed roles, from traditional American culture, and at times an attempt to break out of one's skin through drug use. Thus the opposition youth sprang not from material deprivation or discrimination, but from affluence and privilege. By 1970 three-quarters of American college students thought basic changes were needed to improve American society, while only 19 percent thought the system was headed in the right direction (Keniston 1971: viii).

The development sketched here indicates that since 1960, larger and larger numbers of college students have become increasingly disenchanted, not only with their immediate campus environment, but also with society at large. This disenchantment is reflected in, and to some extent fostered by, increasing ghettoization of these people. Lofland (1968) has suggested using the term "youth ghetto" for large communities occupied mainly by college students. These communities are characterized by poor housing, high rents, and price gouging. The residents are highly mobile, geographically heterogeneous, in turmoil, and often in conflict with the police. This polarization between youth and the rest of society has been called alienation. These alienated young are for some (Mead 1970; Roszak 1969; Keniston 1971; Reich 1971) the most significant source of contemporary radical dissent and cultural innovation.

The term alienation has been variously defined and over-used. It has been used to describe the separation of spirit from nature, man's loss of relationship to his work, his loss of sanity, disillusionment with politics, a "deadening of man's sensitivity to man" (Roszak 1969: 58), and various other conditions. Rather than try to disentangle the various meanings of such an ill-defined word, Keniston's (1971: 174) definition of alienation as ". . . an explicit rejection of what are seen as dominant values of the surrounding society" will be used. It is a rejection of the trusting, optimistic, sociocentric view of society. In youth this rejection and subsequent hostility has been called the generation gap.[1]

Keniston (1968) describes the youthful dissenters as small in numbers but

---

[1] For a very strong viewpoint on generational conflict today see Mead (1970: 49): "In a sense all of us who were born and reared before the 1940s are immigrants. Like first generation pioneers, we were reared to have skills and values that are only partly appropriate to this new time, but we are the elders who still command the techniques of government and power."

powerful in effect because they have uncovered previously unrecognized contradictions in technological society. His studies indicate that alienated students have a distrust going beyond a "low view of human nature [and that] they also believe that intimacy ends in disillusion,[2] that attachment to a group entails the loss of individuality, and that all appearances are untrustworthy. Nor can American culture be trusted; it is mechanical, boring, trashy, cheap, conformist and dull." (Keniston 1968: 177)

It would be a mistake to assume that youth constitutes a homogeneous entity. Instead we witness cleavages within the youth category which can be as deep as those that separate youth from other age groups. Thanks to the media, we now recognize hippies, yippies, Jesus freaks, skin heads, satan-cultists, Hell's Angels, drop-outs, and various other groups. Although these groups share certain specific concerns, their interests and ideologies are indeed diverse. An indication of this diversity is provided by different communes. Some are organic farms, others formed as families, or to experiment with drugs or group sex, or to organize politically. In general, different groups pursue a broad spectrum of alternative life styles and ideas reflecting disillusionment with society.

This disillusionment is not confined to those young people who are free to pursue alternative life styles. In fact, *Manpower*, a U.S. Department of Labor journal (*Boston Sunday Globe*, February 13, 1971, *Parade Magazine*, p. 3), reports that among workers under thirty years of age, both turnover rates and absenteeism are increasing. Workers talk back to their bosses and are no longer willing to accept traditional authoritarian ways. The survey shows that young workers, as they become better educated, experience less satisfaction with their jobs. This lack of satisfaction overshadows even financial considerations, a position totally foreign to their elders.

The composite picture shows young people who share a common element of disillusionment with society. This sense of discontent seems strongest among college youth, but in some attenuated form it is also present among others. What are its roots?

Awareness of loneliness, of isolation, is one of the most pervasive experiences of the contemporary world. The exploration of loneliness and isolation through movies, novels, and the news media have made the word alienation commonplace. The problems of individual isolation and the fact of alienation in today's world is the basis of existentialist philosophy, giving this philosophy great appeal for youth.

The alienation of individuals is Marx and Engels' (1939: 74–5) chief criticism of capitalism. For Freud (1936), it is separation and fear of separation that triggers much anxiety. The fear of loneliness and insignificance is a central theme in Fromm's (1941) *Escape from Freedom* and in Durkheim's (1951) and Merton's (1949) analysis of anomie.

Harry Stack Sullivan (1953) thinks that many contemporary personal, psychological difficulties have their roots not in the individual, but in social pathology. Furthermore, he sees these social pathologies as cumulative, so that the common lot is worsening with time. Marcuse (1962), who is widely read by college students, sees a coercive character in modern society and says that Freud's insistence on the

---

[2] Meerloo (1956: 163–64), a psychoanalyst, says that for many people fear of human relations is greater than fear of death; they fear taking the emotional responsibility of having an emotional involvement with other human beings.

inherent hostility between individual desires and social demands correctly describes the alienation of the person in capitalist society. Marcuse has made a point of the extent to which society represses human potential. According to Erikson (1968: 23), "The identity crises in individual life and contemporary crises in historical development cannot be separated because the two help define each other and are truly relative to each other."

These ideas indicate that alienation stems from an interaction between psychological and sociological phenomena. In order to better understand this interaction we will now move to the psychological level—that of identity.

THE UNDERLYING PROBLEM: IDENTITY

Since the original publication in 1950 of Erikson's *Childhood and Society*, the term "identity" has come into wide usage among such social scientists as Parsons (1951), Lynd (1961), Burton and Whiting (1961), Goodenough (1963), Turner (1964), Garfinkle (1965), and Schwartz and Merton (1968). Erikson's recognition of the search for identity can be regarded as strategic today as was the study of sexuality in Freud's time. His recognition of self-conscious youth playing out identity problems on a large scale renders his observations extremely comprehensible in terms of understanding the behavior of today's youth. Many young people today are neither psychological adolescents nor sociological adults; they are in a stage of life that lacks any clear definition. These young people who form the core of youth culture in America tend to be between the ages of eighteen and thirty (although they may be of any chronological age, witness the gray-haired hippies scattered among them).

Erikson's choice of the word identity is double edged to indicate the interplay between the inner and outer world of an individual. Goffman (1967a: 31) also uses a "double definition of self; the self as an image pieced together from the expressive implications of the full flow of events in an undertaking; and the self as a kind of player in a ritual game who copes honorably or dishonorably, diplomatically." For Erikson, however, it is never this clearly defined, but has numerous connotations: "At one time it seemed to refer to a conscious sense of individual uniqueness, at another to an unconscious striving for a continuity of experience and at a third a solidarity with a group's ideals" (Erikson 1968: 208). By implication he includes in his meaning of identity the self as subject and object. What is clear, then, is that the self stands in constant interaction with its environment, and that in this interaction, identity synthesis takes place. Identity, as Erikson presents it, is not to be equated with autonomy, since autonomy lacks the double direction of identity.

The complex, bi-faceted nature of an ambivalent tension that sometimes develops in the interaction of self and society can lead to identity confusion or a poorly developed sense of identity. If a person cannot find aspects of his social situation with which he can identify, he will find it almost impossible to develop his own selfhood.[3] Identity confusion can lead to incapacity in the development of psychosocial relationships with others, whether in friendship, sexual encounters, or in

---

[3] Erikson states that many Americans find it difficult to cope with the tension demanded by polarities in American culture: ". . . the never-ceasing necessity of remaining tentative in order to be free to take the next step" (1946: 388–9).

cooperative creative endeavors. This may result in a deep sense of isolation and feelings of personal inadequacy.

Erikson (1950; 1968) postulates eight stages in the development of the individual personality, each of which involves a characteristic conflict and a possible crisis. The eight stage-defining conflicts are, in their proper order (Erikson 1968: 94):

1. trust   vs   mistrust
2. autonomy   vs   shame, doubt
3. initiative   vs   guilt
4. industry   vs   inferiority
5. identity   vs   identity confusion
6. intimacy   vs   isolation
7. generativity   vs   stagnation, self-absorption
8. integrity   vs   disgust, despair

Any stage may lead to difficulties if its particular conflict is not resolved in a way that is constructive for the growing individual. If the conflict is resolved, it opens new possibilities for increased development of the personality and increased strength of identity. All stages are systematically related to the others. Each stage depends on appropriate development in proper sequence of all previous stages; and each stage-defining conflict exists in some form before its crisis time appears.[4] This scheme explicitly recognizes the importance of shifting social relations, the surplus energy inherent in each stage, and the mutual involvement of self and society.[5]

Erikson (1968: passim) makes it clear that identity is the critical crisis of youth and that adulthood, although it should represent an emergence from the identity period and go beyond it, often does not. Thus, every basic conflict of childhood lives on, in some form, in the adult. For Erikson a firm sense of identity marks the end of the adolescent youth process; but the development of identity may continue for some individuals throughout life.

Inspection of the list of conflicts given above reveals that the items in the right-hand column relate to a rejection of the dominant values of society and to the negative connotations implicit in the phenomenon of alienation. (Recall Keniston's findings from his studies of college youth.) Thus, the unresolved conflicts in youth correspond to what we have called alienation and give us the deeper level conflicts and crises which may arise if young people cannot find their sense of identity within their own culture.

It is during youth that people should be developing a sense of identity, but it is also during this period that modern society often fails them. The failure is found in the lack of formal rituals, lack of positive models and identifications, and lack of ideology.

Often a youth is what Turner (1964: 107) calls "betwixt and between." He is in a "liminal" (Turner 1969: 94) stage where "he passes through a cultural realm that has few or none of the attributes of the past or coming state." The very ambiguity of this stage plus its possible prolongation in our society hinders rather

---

[4] Erikson's formulation is intended to complement Freud's theory of development with its emphasis on sexual conflicts and maturation.

[5] In *Young Man Luther* (1958) and *Gandhi's Truth* (1969), Erikson demonstrates how life crises and contemporary crises are mutually interdependent.

than enhances an individual's identity development. In modern society, a lack of formalized rituals initiating on into adulthood[6] has been replaced by a youth period. This period, while not obviously transitional, is more of a waiting period in which the indivdual is supposed to prepare himself for adulthood. Erikson's (1968: 128–132) observation of an apparent unwillingness to grow up leads him to believe that our youth culture is a psychological suspension of adulthood. Youth culture should provide an opportunity to develop an adult identity and to serve the positive function of resolving generational discontinuity, but it often does not. An important psychological function of a sense of identity is to provide a sense of inner continuity,[7] to bind together the past, the present, and the future into a coherent whole.

Identity is not just given by society. Rather, each person must make his unique synthesis of the models, identifications, and ideals offered by society. Never before has such freedom of choice been available in regard to work, styles of life, and beliefs. Youth may well be victims of the dilemma of overchoice[8] (Toffler 1970: 241). It becomes obvious that the proliferation of models, identifications, and ideals (often incompatible with one another) makes the task of constructing a coherent identity a difficult one. In some cases it is perhaps impossible to achieve.

Childhood and youth are often romanticized in modern society. The comparison with this romantic stereotype renders the adult world of settling down, growing up, and assuming responsibilities something for youth to fear. Childhood is fantasy, play, spontaneity, nonconformity, experimentation, and change. Adulthood, on the other hand, means forfeiture of these qualities in favor of specialization, monotony, conformity, commitment, and lack or incapability of change. The adult deceleration of personal change can represent to youth an unconscious equation with death or nonbeing, a frightening prospect indeed.

Adulthood today is a role little better defined than that of youth. We are seldom sure precisely what is required in order to be an adult. Even Erikson (1968: 33) can only present adulthood as a problem: "how to take care of those to whom one finds oneself committed as one emerges from the identity period and to whom one now owes their identity." Moreover, even such seemingly universal adult roles as mother and father are amorphous and changing. Many thinking adults, such as those represented by the National Organizaiton of Women and Zero Population Growth, seek to redefine these roles.

It becomes clear that if so-called "adults" are confused about their adult identities and role definition, the same general confusion will be transmitted to their children. For youth, therefore, the development of a coherent adult identity and the resolution of generational discontinuities is becoming more difficult.

Much of what has been said about adult roles also applies to ideology. Ideology provides a basic outlook on the world which can orient one's actions in adult life

[6] See Van Gennep (1960), Mead (1970).

[7] Erikson (1950: 227–8) notes that for adolescents in our society "role diffusion," trying out a variety of cultural roles, is an attempt to find in these roles a confirmation or a substitute for inner continuity.

[8] An example cited by Roszak (1969: 64) is a Congress on the Dialectics of Liberation held in London (1967) to work out priorities of psychic and social liberation, attended by New Left revolutionaries, existential psychiatrists, Black Power spokesmen, and Allen Ginsberg. The latter, with his following, insisted on chanting "Hare Krsna." Priorities never did get established.

(Erikson 1968: 133–34). The same adult world that fails to provide youth with a clear-cut definition of adult roles also fails in the ideological realm. The conventional churches lack an ideology capable of inspiring commitment in either young or old. Many adults do not bother to attend church, and the religious behavior of those who do appears hypocritical. Their involvement is shallow, requiring little more than Sunday church attendance and lip service to an ideology that has little application in everyday life. Many adults seem committed only to the secular values of money making and to a faith in scientific technology.

The identity confusion generated by the structural and ideological models presented to youth is related to the fluidity inherent in both. Individuals should be able to alleviate their identity confusion by placing themselves in a well-defined and rigid structural and ideological situation. Such a situation would have some of the elements of what Goffman (1961) calls a "total institution," elements which will be discussed in the following section.

The ISKCON temple provides a total-institutional setting which allows its members a well-defined structural and ideological situation into which they can fit themselves. It creates a social situation in which they can realize their identities, thereby eliminating much of the ambiguity which is generated by modern society. An ISKCON temple also provides formal rites, positive identifications and models, and an ideology, all of which are lacking in modern society. The temple setting can also help resolve some of the conflicts of the youth stage on the sides of trust, autonomy, initiative, industry, identity, intimacy, generativity, and integrity.

A POSSIBLE SOLUTION: THE ISKCON TEMPLE

It is the contention of this work that those young people who turn to ISKCON seek an ideology and life style which they believe the matrix society does not offer them. Moreover, it is necessary to understand whether one's experiences within ISKCON promote or retard one's psychological development. Therefore, this work will attempt to explore the peculiar problems of social and self-identity which lead today's youth to conversion into ISKCON and entrance into an ISKCON temple.

Entrance into the temple provides a crucial self-degradation ritual whereby many disoriented individuals find new identities as devotees. It is also an educational arena where an individual is socialized into the terminology and the strategies necessary to life in a temple setting apart from the dominant society. Repeated association with other devotees and withdrawal from the parent society serve to strengthen the culture of Krsna Consciousness as it presently exists.

A Krsna-conscious temple setting can be considered a total institution as Goffman defines it in *Asylums*—"as a place of residence and work where a number of like-situated individuals, cut off from the wider society for an appreciable period of time, together lead an enclosed formally administered round of life" (Goffman 1961: xiii). Common features of total institutions, which differ from the "basic social arrangements" in modern society, are:

1. All aspects of life are conducted in the same place and under the same single authority.

Chanting on the street.

2. Each phase of the member's daily activity is carried on in the immediate company of a large batch of others, all of whom are treated alike and required to do the same thing together.
3. All phases of the day's activities are tightly scheduled . . . the whole sequence of activities being imposed from above by a system of explicit formal rulings and a body of officials.
4. The various enforced activities are brought together into a rational plan purportedly designed to fill the official aims of the institution. (Goffman 1961: 6)

Goffman (1961: 12) also suggests that these institutions are "forcing houses for changing persons; each is a natural experiment on what can be done to the self." In everyday life each person presents an image of himself (this image equates with Erikson's term identity) which is perceived by others who, on the basis of this perception, interact with him in a complex manner. As we shall see, in a total institution these interactions tend to be very different from those in society at large.

Following Goodenough (1963: 178), we must recognize the fact that "a person's identity as he perceives it, his self image, does not necessarily coincide with his identity as perceived by others." This recalls the previous separation of an individual's identity into the personal and social components. One's social identity, then, is comprised of personal judgments made by others plus one's current roles and statuses in society. Each party in an interaction presents an image of himself and each defers to the other's demeanor avoiding unnecessary challenges and contradictions (Goffman 1967a).

Total institutions violate these customs by refusing to defer to the new member's presentation of self. In ISKCON, for example, one's self-concept (identity) is directly attacked by depriving him of the deference which his accustomed demeanor brought him outside the temple. Moreover, he is deprived of those accoutrements of his prior status which he employed in his presentation of self; clothing, hair style, personal possessions, and freedom of association. Once broken, the self is theoretically reconstituted by conformity with new deferences in the form of special status conferred on the individual as he progresses in ISKCON. Naturally, an individual's personality has a history prior to his entrance into the temple. This history simultaneously limits and expands opportunities for new self-definitions.

In summary, the search for identity, for a definition of self, is one of the main concerns of youth today. Young people appear preoccupied with personal consciousness and experimentation; the dropped-out, self-absorbed individual sunk in a narcotic stupor or lost in ecstatic contemplation is a common enough sight. It is to this task of remodeling themselves that the devotees of ISKCON dedicate themselves, attempting to strike through ideology to the level of consciousness in order to transform the deepest sense of self, relationships with others, and even their environment. Perhaps these young people do not have the fortitude necessary to carry through the epochal transformations they seek, but it is certain they do not want less.

2 / A guru comes from India

I offer my humble obeisances unto His Divine Grace Prabhupada A. C. Bhaktivedanta Swami . . .
who, alone, in his seventieth year, threw family, society, friendship, love to the
wind, left mother India and set sail around the earth to foreign, unknown
shores because his spiritual leader spoke to him in a dream.
who landed in Manhattan with saffron robes, a suitcase and seven dollars and
wondered at "mayas" skyscrapers and empty noisy dreams. (Hayagriva dasa
Adhikari)

A. C. Bhaktivedanta Swami was born Abhay Charan De on September 1,
1896, in Calcutta, India. Of his father, Gour Mohon De, he has said: "He was a
pure devotee of Krsna, who raised me as a Krsna-conscious child from the beginning of my life. He was kind to me and I imbibed from him the ideas that were
later solidified by my spiritual master, the eternal father."

In 1920 he terminated his education after majoring in philosophy, English, and
economics at the University of Calcutta. Because of his involvement in Gandhi's
national noncooperation movement he would not accept any formal diploma.[1]
After leaving the university, Abhay Charan De managed a large chemical concern.
In 1922, he met Sri Srimad Bhaktisiddhanta Saraswati Gosvami Maharaja, who, in
1918, founded the Gaudiya Vaisnava Maths (temples) in India, Berlin, and
London.[2] Saraswati liked this charming, educated young man and injected in him
the idea of preaching the message of Lord Caitanya throughout the world.

Bhaktivedanta recalled the key to approaching his spiritual master: "When I
first started going to see my Guru Maharaja, he said of me, 'This boy hears very
nicely; he does not go away; so I shall make him a disciple.' That was my qualification, or whatever you may call it. I would simply ask when Guru Maharaja
would speak, then I'd sit down and go on hearing . . . others would disperse, I'd not
disperse. So he remarked, 'This boy is interested to hear.' Because I was serious in

[1] Bhaktivedanta Swami now says of Ghandi: "Although he was considered a mahatma, still
the intoxication of materialistic life caught him up. Although he got his desire, although the
Britishers left India, still he would not give up his politics. That is the way of material life.
Men refuse to retire until they are killed by the laws of material nature . . . he (Ghandi)
continued to meddle with politics until his assistants became disgusted and his assassination
followed." (*Back to Godhead*, No. 42, p. 6.)
[2] By the time of Saraswati's death, there were sixty-four Gaudiya Vaisnava Maths established: sixty-two of the maths were in India, one was in Berlin, and one in London. After
Saraswati's death, a conflict split the movement into several factions, each recognizing a
different guru.

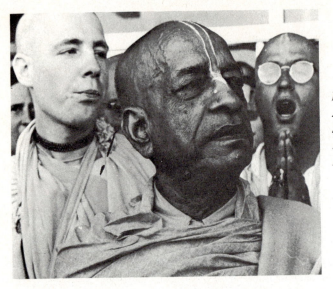

His Divine Grace A. C. Bhaktivedanta Swami Prabhupada. Photo courtesy of ISKCON.

hearing, I am now serious about kirtana, which means speaking or preaching. If one has heard nicely, one will speak nicely."

In 1933, Abhay Charan De was formally initiated at Allahabad, and in 1936, just days before Saraswati's death, he claims to have been specifically ordered by his guru to spread Krsna Consciousness to the English-speaking people of the West.[3]

Back to Godhead magazine was started in 1944 with Abhay Charan De serving as editor-in-chief. It is still being published monthly by the American ISKCON disciples whom Bhaktivedanta recruited in the United States. Bhaktivedanta remained in the Gaudiya Vaisnava Society after Saraswati's death, and he was initiated as Bhaktivedanta in 1947. Bhaktivedanta was a grhastra (householder) devotee, who lived outside the math with his family. He was very active in the movement, helping Saraswati to establish some maths in Bengal, India. In 1954 he became vanaprastha, retired from family life, became known as A. C. Bhaktivedanta Swami, and broke all connection with his wife and family.[4] He was able to do this because his children were grown annd his wife was a rich man's daughter who owned property. By 1962 Bhaktivedanta had become successful in starting his own society called The League of Devotees in Vrndavana, Delhi, and was publishing scriptural texts. In 1965, at the advanced age of seventy, Bhaktivedanta arrived in the United States to fulfill his master's sacred mission. His only possessions were seven dollars,[5] a letter of introduction to an Indian family in Pennsylvania, and a suitcase with some volumes of his beloved Vedic scriptures.

[3] Many devotees have told me that Saraswati came to Bhaktivedanta in a dream and ordered him to spread Krsna Consciousness to the western world.

[4] Of his family connections Bhaktivedanta has said: "Finally I have left my family . . . now I have found that in the past twenty years they are living and I am also living. They are neither dying nor suffering in my absence, and I am not suffering in their absence. Indeed by Krsna's grace I now have better family members, such nice children in a foreign country who are taking such good care of me that I could never expect such good care from my own children."

[5] Bhaktivedanta's first journey to the United States was financed by Srimati Sumati Morarji, a woman "industrialist" and owner of Scindia Steamship Lines. Srimati Morarji is reputed to be the richest woman in India.

KRSNA COMES TO SECOND AVENUE

Once in New York Bhaktivedanta was helped out by "hashish-yogis," who he met on the street and who kindly gave him shelter. He then set up quarters in a lower East Side store front with what money he was able to beg on the streets and "trusted Krsna to bring the next month's rent." Each day he went out to Tompkins Park seeking devotees and invited those that he met in the park to come to his evening classes until he had some disciples to lead out for daily chanting in the streets. Slowly, but surely, Bhaktivedanta had found enough new devotees to hold his first fire sacrifice ceremony to initiate a dozen members in his store front temple. He trained these few disciples to preach, to beg, to cook, to chant on the streets, and to carry on the work he started.

On a sudden invitation he took a jet to San Francisco, telling his New York disciples he'd return in two weeks, and after four months' absence he laughed and said, "You have not reckoned a day of Brahma."[6] In San Francisco's Avalon ballroom he lectured, chanted, danced with Allen Ginsberg, Moby Grape, Grateful Dead, Big Brother, and Timothy Leary. After his return to New York, he suffered a stroke, but recovered rapidly. He then began traveling around the United States, India, and Japan. Today he still travels throughout the world, stopping at different ISKCON centers "to guide his disciples through daily life."

In July 1966 the International Society for Krsna Consciousness (ISKCON) was formally incorporated. It is said that Saraswati once drew a picture of a mrdanga (drum used on sankirtana) and beside it, a printing press. He said the mrdanga could be heard for several blocks, but a printing press could be heard around the world. ISKCON press was established for the exclusive printing of Bhaktivedanta's books. As he has said, "When you become self-realized you automatically write volumes of books." It is also claimed by Bhaktivedanta that the literature he produces is authorized by the disciplic succession descending from Krsna himself.[7]

I KISS YOUR LOTUS FEET

The spiritual master, whose full title is His Divine Grace A. C. Bhaktivedanta Swami Prabhupada, is called Prabhupada, meaning "One at whose feet many masters sit." He is worshipped as a pure devotee of the Lord, the latest in the long line of disciplic succession extending back to Krsna's appearance on earth five thousand years ago. Prabhupada does not reside in any one place, but travels from temple to temple. Many of the devotees have never met him; yet, through voluminous personal correspondence, he has provided the kind of a strong paternal presence that they seem to relish in their daily lives. His secretary answers the letters of the devotees with words of warning, instruction or praise in mundane as well as

---

[6] "Each day and each night of Brahma lasts one thousand years of the Gods, and each year of the Gods corresponds to twelve thousand years of men" (Zaehner 1968: 61).

[7] The reader will observe that in the disciplic succession (Appendix I) there are not enough men to bridge the five-thousand-year time span claimed for the disciplic succession (parampara). Bhaktivedanta accounts for any discrepancies by telling the devotees that in days past men lived longer and had perfect memories and that men today do not have these qualities because they live in the age of kali-yuga (the age of quarrel), where men are more fallen and degenerate.

religious matters. He initiates new devotees through the mail, sending each his new "spiritual" name and explaining its auspicious meanings. He also sends regular taped monologues on the philosophy of Krsna Consciousness, spoken in a heavily accented voice,[8] to which the devotees listen each night as they sip bowls of warm, sweetened milk. The devotees mimic many of Prabhupada's speech mannerisms and expressions and use them in everyday speech; they also love to ape him in quoting "scripture" whenever they are able.

When asked how one recognizes a spiritual master, most devotees say he simply emerges. One of his first devotees spoke of meeting Prabhupada. He felt attracted to this strange man he discovered chanting bare chested and alone in Tompkins Park. "At first I thought Prabhupada was a Buddhist monk. I was attracted to him because he was kind, so I began going to the classes he gave in his storefront temple although at first I could hardly understand his English. Prabhupada always spoke of a spiritual master and his own spiritual master until finally, from my study of the *Bhagavad-gita*, I realized he was a bona fide spiritual master." From another devotee: "An incarnation never says 'I am an incarnation,' nor does an avatara canvass for students. Because of his special qualities he is automatically accepted." Still another devotee said of his spiritual master, "A bona fide spiritual master is not an ordinary person. If a disciple does not understand the transcendental nature of his spiritual master, then it is better for him not to accept a spiritual master. Accepting a spiritual master means to surrender everything 100 percent to him. You cannot argue or debate with him. You can only surrender and inquire . . . Krsna says in the Eleventh Canto of the *Srimad-Bhagavatam*, 'The spiritual master must be accepted not only as my representative but as my very self. He must never be considered on the same level as an ordinary human being' . . . I therefore prostrate myself like a stick in the dust of the lotus feet of his Divine Grace A. C. Bhaktivedanta Swami Prabhupada."

According to a female devotee, "I worship Srila Prabhupada, the real father and mother of us all, at whose lotus feet I am always taking shelter . . . the golden Lord and lover, who is always pouring forth transcendental nectar." Another explains, "The orphans you have nursed to life bow down their heads in thankfulness. I thank you for fathering so many Vaisnava God-brothers and sisters and I can learn at their feet; they who are learning to be worthy of the regal name Vaisnava."

This is but a sampling of the primary means by which devotees express devotion and submission to their spiritual master. Their relationship to him is, of necessity, one of distant devotion for all except a small number of hand-picked devotees who have become Prabhupada's "personal servants" and stay with him always. Any person (devotee or not) must request an appointment with Bhaktivedanta from one of his personal servants before seeing him. In many cases the request is granted, but it may be refused or later cancelled. When I asked to speak personally with the spiritual master, my request was granted and I was told to return at ten o'clock the next morning. The next morning promptly at ten I appeared. I was told that Prabhupada was napping and that if I wanted to see him I must wait until the following morning. His servants were aware that I had made a special trip to New

---

[8] In the words of a nondevotee visitor, "I could hardly understand what he was saying. He spoke half English, half Bengali, and the Bengali was more understandable."

York to meet Prabhupada and that I had limited time, but I was still told to return the next day or come back during the following week. As usual, Bhaktivedanta remained closeted in his private quarters during most of his stay at the temple. He would appear occasionally in the temple, or go out for a walk with a chosen few, but rarely did he mingle with his devotees. The devotees, on the other hand, exist hoping to see him and dreaming that during his visits he will smile upon them. His carefully maintained distance inspires even more devotion because, like the Lord, this parental figure remains inaccessible.[9]

There is little doubt that Bhaktivedanta's life style has changed radically since his humble beginnings in New York. Today he is always accompanied by a retinue of personal servants who cater to his every whim. It is the duty of his servants to serve the guru his food and drink, to shave him, to massage him, to care for his clothing, to chauffer him, and to handle all of his money matters. He stays in plush quarters which are especially prepared for him in the different temples he chooses to visit. In New York he is driven around in a luxurious Cadillac car. Still, Bhaktivedanta's life seems less flamboyant and simpler than other popular gurus. An observer, Rev. Frederick J. Murphy (1973: 1–2), compares the well-known Guru Maharaj Ji to Bhaktivedanta:

> All in all, there is an unmistakable sense of disappointment in listening to Guru Maharaj Ji, the so-called Perfect Master, disappointment in the content of the message which until now has enthralled some five million Indians and 40,000 Americans. There is disappointment in the elaborate lifestyle which has made the guru suspect to Indian custom officials and which is beginning to erode his following. There is little of the typical mark of Indian renunciation in the lifestyle of Maharaj Ji.
>
> India has always produced her saints, but in vain do you look at Maharaj Ji for some of the qualifications that surround, for example, the life of A. C. Bhaktivedanta, the founder of the International Society for Krsna Consciousness, whose translation and commentary on the "Bhagavad Gita" has a foreword by Thomas Merton, and whose followers, however much we may worry about their stability and endurance, adhere to a demanding discipline. It remains to be seen whether Guru Maharaj Ji will be able to sustain his credibility in the months ahead.

Bhaktivedanta does not ever make a direct claim to be God, only to being His representative on earth.[10] There are many ambiguities in Vedic scripture and in Bhaktivedanta's interpretations of scripture on this subject. When asked directly about his status the devotees usually hedge by making statements such as, "He is simultaneously one and different." (This point will be discussed in the final chapter; for the present it will suffice to note that the ambiguity exists.) For his followers, however, he has become the authority figure that many of them never had, plus the mediator with God. A surface impression is maintained by the distance and inaccessibility of the man himself who represents authority, love, shelter, and

---

[9] It is interesting to note that Bhaktivedanta (1970a: 13) says, "Similarly in dreams I sometimes find that I have become a king. Oh, there are so many riches and so much opulence. Then, as soon as the dream is over, I come home and all is gone."

[10] Compare Bhaktivedanta to Meher Baba, another guru, who claimed to be God, the avatara (Needleman 1972), or Maharaj Ji, the fifteen-year-old child God (Balyogeshwar), who enjoyed so much popularity in the United States in 1973.

the model of "godliness in man." He promises to bring them "home—back to Godhead!"

If the surface impressions of Bhaktivedanta lead one to think he is primarily sweetness and light, a closer look will illustrate how sharp is his demand on his followers and how great is their struggle to come closer to him. This is clearly expressed in a poem written to him by an anonymous devotee:

> O Savior of all the worlds,
> Srila Prabhupada, it is you!
>
> Some men worship cats and dogs,
> Some sacrifice their all to fleeting sex;
> What mercy You bestow to all who take
> Devotional Service, eternal, O Divine Grace.
>
> Where are You going, Srila Prabhupada?
> Back to that realm from when You came?
> Strike me or kill me—that I beg,
> But never leave me, O Divine Grace.
>
> The pollution You see is all my own;
> How painful to one so pure.
> How can You forever absorb my sins,
> Yet remain forever without sin?
>
> Such patience, O Holy Father, no one can deserve;
> But if You do not dry up my filthy mind,
> What sun is left uncontaminate?
> I have no other shelter than You!

The struggle and surrender to this spiritual master is harsh and will be further explored in a later chapter. But through poems and lip service around the temple, the impression of great love and surrender to the holy master is expressed. His disciples tell of the love and kindness they feel radiating from him and of their great devotion to him. The poems and letters written to their master fulfill their vital need to feel closer to Prabhupada; to disobey, mistrust, or betray him is rejection of the love and mercy he has offered them.

A GURU—THE DIRECT ROUTE TO GOD

The devotees seem to be preoccupied with what is bona fide or real about their guru and how he differs from other "bogey yogis." He presents them with definite answers to this question. He gives them the authority they demand by claiming direct unbroken disciplic succession from Krsna and citing the authority of Vedic literature. Prabhupada claims that his whole "life mission is to faithfully pass on the understanding of Krsna Consciousness without distortion," and that the only way this can be done is through the descending disciplic process (parampara): "The absolute truth is beyond the reach of mundane speculation or scholarship." For this reason his first publication, called the Bhagavad-gita As It Is, includes not only his translation, but is also generously sprinkled with purports which explain the *exact* meaning of each verse. Hence, there need be no speculation on the part of his following. A devotee expressed it this way:

> Due to imperfect senses and due to a tendency to cheat, which are characteristic of every man, the scriptures are better received through a perfectly realized medium. If one wants to study chemistry, mathematics, geography, or physics, he does not simply check out a chemistry or physics book out of the library and sit down and begin reading. No, he buys the books, attends the lectures in the university, takes notes of the professor's lectures, does the assigned reading, takes the examination, and finally writes a thesis under the guidance of his professor. If mundane science is so difficult that one needs a teacher in addition to textbooks, how much more does one need a teacher to understand the mystical interior process of self-realization? So just as professors and textbooks are necessary for the understanding of a material science, the guru and scriptures are necessary for the understanding of the spiritual science of Krsna. Therefore, Lord Krsna says in the *Bhagavad-gita* (130), "Just try to learn the truth by approaching a spiritual master. Inquire from him submissively and render service unto him. The self-realized soul can impart knowledge unto you because he has seen the truth."

Since only God can establish a bona fide religion, this insistence on the authority of the scripture is meant both to discourage people from inventing their own religions and to warn others against following false gurus. The specific qualifications of a bona fide spiritual master are outlined in the Eleventh Canto of the *Srimad-Bhagavatam* (known in the literature as the *Bhagavata Purana*) as follows:

> He follows scriptural injunctions very rigidly.
> His character is perfect. (He follows the twenty-six qualifications of a devotee mentioned in the Vedic scripture.)
> He follows the principles of devotional service.
> He is fully conversant with the Vedic scriptures.
> He has conquered the six sense-gratifying agents, namely the tongue, genitals, belly, anger, mind, and words.

It is important to understand the position of the guru as a pure devotee. As was stated earlier, he is a representative of God who never claims to be God. Because he has knowledge of God, he is paid all the respect ordinarily given to God. Although it is stated that the spiritual master is "the external manifestation of Krsna," he should not be considered mundane or material. In their daily prayers to the spiritual master the devotees say,

> We offer our respectful obeisances to our spiritual master Srila Prabhupada who is most dear to Lord Krsna on this earth, having taken shelter of His Lotus Feet.

Rupa Gosvami (Bhaktivedanta 1970b: xxxii) summarizes the definition of a pure devotee: "His service is favorable and always in relation to Krsna." Krsna (Bhaktivedanta 1968: 315) himself states that one who explains the *Bhagavad-gita* is most dear to him.

The distinction is always made between the devotee of God and God himself, but a neophyte devotee should respect the servants of God as God. Such servants of God are called mahatmas (great souls). The standard quality of the servants of God is that they canvass people to become devotees of the Lord, and they never tolerate the blasphemy of being called God. For example, Lord Caitanya[11] (be-

---

[11] See Chapter 3, p. 25.

lieved to be the most recent major incarnation of Krsna) was God himself according to the scriptures, but he played the part of an ordinary devotee. When a person addressed him as God, he used to block his ears with his hands and murmur the name of Visnu. Still there is some confusion generated as to who the spiritual master actually is. In the *Nectar of Devotion*, Bhaktivedanta (1970b: 59) quotes Krsna as saying,

> The spiritual master must be accepted not only as my representative but as my very self. He must never be considered on the same level as an ordinary human being. One should never be envious of the spiritual master as one may be envious of an ordinary man.

The spiritual master is eternally perfect because his birth, his deeds, and his activities are all transcendental. Krsna has sixty-four transcendental qualities, say the devotees, while a pure devotee has only the first fifty-five qualities. The devotees like to say that Krsna and the spiritual master are like two rails of the same track. The original spiritual master is Krsna himself and the disciplic succession comes from him. So it is with the pure devotee, who is in a unique position to understand and explain the *Bhagavad-gita* and Krsna Consciousness, for he knows the *Bhagavad-gita* as it is.

In spite of the strict discipline that they follow, the devotees insist that chanting the Hare Krsna mantra is the easiest and most direct route to salvation. Doesn't Prabhupada always tell them, "Why walk up to the top of the Empire State Building when you can take the elevator and see the same view?" It is because Bhaktivedanta is the sole possessor of the absolute truth that he is in a position to answer any question that can be asked. Although some of his answers may seem absurd, many people are nevertheless impressed by the courage with which he faces the unanswerable. The devotees had been asking for years without receiving what they believed to be satisfactory answers. Prabhupada may be the first person to have answered these questions. To understand the susceptibility of so many young people to ISKCON's teaching, we must now examine the philosophy of the movement. Later we shall explore the almost fanatical devotion of the membership.

3 / Roots in India

I offer my humble obeisances unto His Divine Grace Prabhupada A. C. Bhaktivedanta Swami . . .
   who, always engaged in chanting and celebrating the message of Lord Caitanya,
      sometimes dances in ecstasy and trembles and quivers in his trance,
   who sat quietly beneath a persimmon tree reading Srimad-Bhagavatam and
      musing over the Appalachians.
Who composed Sanskrit odes to the Primeval Spirit whose eternal teenage lips
   play a flute. (Hayagriva dasa Adhikari)

SCRIPTURE: THE IDEOLOGY

It becomes increasingly evident that Krsna-conscious literature is not a literature of any national culture or sectarian religion, nor can it be designated
simply as Hinduism, nor is it occultism. Rather, the writings of His Divine Grace
are addressed to all humanity, for they clearly teach the purpose of the human
form of life and the dangers in misusing this form by failing to cultivate spiritual
knowledge. Such knowledge can alone answer the basic questions of "Who am
I?" "Where do I come from?" "What is the purpose of existence?" and "Where
am I going?" His Divine Grace has founded ISKCON press so that pure knowledge of the culture of Krsna Consciousness can be revealed to the reading
public.[1]

The heart of this pure knowledge is said by the devotees to be contained in
the *Bhagavad-gita* (The Song of God, also known as the *Geetopanisad*) probably
the most popular book in Vedic literature. It can be called the gospel of India
because of its profound influence on the spiritual, cultural, intellectual, and political life of that country today and throughout centuries past. The date of the *Gita*
is generally placed as somewhere between the fifth and second centuries, B.C., and
it is part of a larger work, the *Mahabharata*.[2] In his introduction to the *Gita*, Bhaktivedanta Swami's former American disciple Rayarama says that we can attribute the
Mahabharata to an incarnation of God Vyasadeva, ". . . for it was He who put it

---

[1] Quote by an anonymous devotee from a pamphlet entitled *ISKCON Press Publications
and Media.*
[2] Most scholars agree that the *Gita* was not originally a part of the *Mahabharata*, but
probably existed independently for some time. The *Mahabharata* is not a homogeneous work,
but a collection of narratives. (Prabhavananda and Isherwood 1951: 28) Bhaktivedanta
Swami and ISKCON devotees maintain that it was all written at one time, five thousand
years ago.

into writing. The people of previous times having the capacity for perfect memory of such topics, writing was until then unnecessary" (Bhaktivedanta Swami 1968: 9). Rayarama goes on to say, "The general pattern in translating the *Bhagavad-gita* into English, followed by so many writers of such works, is to brush aside the personality of Krsna in order to make room for the translator's own concepts and philosophies.[3] The history of the *Mahabharata* is taken as quaint mythology, and Krsna becomes a poetic device, an instrument of some anonymous genius' concepts, or, at best, a historical minor personage." For this reason, Bhaktivedanta Swami's first publication issued by ISKCON press is called *Bhagavad-gita As It Is*. This translation claims to make the *Gita* "wholly consistent and comprehensible" and is "necessarily the only translation that can present this scripture in its true terms" (1968: 12).

The *Bhagavad-gita* is for most scholars "the most important, the most influential, and the most luminous of all Hindu scriptures. . . This marks a turning point in Hinduism, for here for the first time a totally new element in Hindu spirituality makes itself felt; the love of God for man and of man for God" (Zaehner 1968: 10). The *Gita* has been embraced by orthodox Hindus as well as modern Hindus of all sects, and even by Mahatma Gandhi, who read the *Gita* daily.

R. C. Zaehner (1968: 6–8) divides Hinduism into four periods.[4]

The earliest of these, of which the principal literary monument is the *Rig-Veda*, is frankly polytheist and clearly akin to the religions of other Indo-European nations. This then develops into (the second period) a pantheistic monism in which the All is seen to be centered on the One or is wholly identified with the One: in its extreme form the individual human soul is identified with the Absolute. In effect this means that the gods are dethroned and the human soul is set up in their place.[5]

The third phase, which is perhaps the most important, is the development within Hinduism of strong monotheistic trends. . . Preoccupation with the liberation of the soul from the bondage of time and matter gives way to a rapt adoration of God, that is to say, of the great traditional gods, Vishnu and Siva, now regarded by their devotees as the supreme Reality and absolute Lord. This religion of loving devotion or bhakti became the real religion of the mass of the people and has remained so ever since. . . .

The fourth phase we are living through today: it is the denial of its formal self and the reassertion of its spiritual essence. This revaluation of Hinduism was prepared by the reform movements of the nineteenth century, but only reached and touched the hearts of the entire Indian people with the advent of a saint who seemed to incarnate all that was best in Hinduism, Mahatma Gandhi.

Bhaktivedanta Swami stresses monotheism (Krsna as the Supreme Personality of Godhead), mukti (liberation), and the bhakti which the *Bhagavad-gita* presents. According to Zaehner, the *Gita* is both the focal point for all later Hinduism and

---

[3] "We do not read any other translations of the *Gita* because they are poison—they don't recognize Krsna as the supreme God" (a woman devotee of ISKCON).

[4] Bhaktivedanta Swami does not agree with Zaehner's analysis of the history of the Vedic tradition. Instead, accepting the statements of the Vedic writings literally, he maintains that a continuous tradition of Vedic knowledge has existed since the Vedas were first spoken.

[5] It is this belief that Bhaktivedanta Swami rails against when he refers to the Mayavadi and Brahmavadi Impersonalists, who do not accept a personal God such as Krsna. He interprets their philosophies as belief that they themselves are God because these impersonalists say that the human soul is the Supreme Absolute. This form of Hinduism is also experiencing a great revival in India and in the western world.

the turning point of early Hinduism away from the original pantheism toward a person-to-person relationship of man to God. He sees the confrontation of Krsna and man (Arjuna) in the *Gita* as the prototype of the relationship to God which is still developing as Hinduism becomes increasingly monotheistic.

In the eleventh century Ramanuja, a theistic philosopher, fused the philosophy of bhakti to his interpretation of the *Gita.* "God imprisons souls in matter only to release them and unite them with himself . . . Moreover, just as the devotee longs for God and loves him, so does God long for the soul . . . God needs the soul as much as the soul 'needs God, and this means that the soul is neither annihilated nor absorbed in the liberated state, but experiences unending and ever increasing love." (Zaehner 1968: 99–100) Ramanuja is the first of the Vaisnava philosophers of whom Madhva, Vallabha, Nimbarka and the followers of Caitanya are the most important. Madhva goes a step further than Ramanuja by calling himself a dualist because he makes a clear distinction between God, who is absolute and independent, and human souls, which are eternal although subject to God. It is from this line of dualists that Bhaktivedanta Swami draws his philosophy following in the footsteps of the eleventh-century Madhva and the fifteenth-century Caitanya (see Appendix I for the disciplic succession).

Bhaktivedanta Swami's philosophy can be placed within the cultural tradition of the Bengali Vaisnavas, which was in some ways complimentary to, and in other ways different from, the great bhakti (devotional) religious movement that "swept across Northern India in the fourteenth to seventeenth centuries A.D. and the older bhakti movements of the south" (Dimock 1966: 41). The Bengali Vaisnava movement probably had its rise in the eleventh or twelfth century A.D. Dimock (1966: 42) postulates an unknown, possibly oral, source for the tradition.

The most significant figure of the Bengal movement and its greatest practitioner was Caitanya (1496–1583). The revival of devotional religion he inspired was so powerful that during his lifetime, and for a while after his death, it encompassed the greater part of eastern India. According to Dimock (1966: 43) Caitanya read Vaisnava texts and became the leader of the Krsna-bhakti in Eastern India. Caitanya introduced kirtana[6] (chanting the name and praises of Krsna), which he considered the most powerful method for bringing about a frame of mind proper for religious devotion in an age conducive to mental distraction. Caitanya was not the originator but the revivalist, since Vaisnavite movements were known in Bengal for at least three centuries before his time. Even during his lifetime some believed him to be an avatara (incarnation) of Krsna, while others believed him to be Krsna himself. Caitanya was not an academic theologian and wrote only eight devotional verses in his lifetime. Dimock (1966: 44) says that Caitanya was not so absorbed in his devotion that he was unable to see the potential power of the movement he led. For this reason he commissioned six theologians, the six Gosvamis,[7] to shape the formal doctrine of the sect. The six Gosvamis, who did the major job of codifying the doctrine and ritual, were scholarly men and wrote in Sanskrit. They were eager to prove that the Krsna of the Bhagavata is himself the

---

[6] There are three principal varieties of kirtana (also called sankirtana): 1. Dancing and group chanting of religious lyrics which celebrate the story of Krsna; 2. Repetitive chanting of the names of the deity; and 3. Street processionals with chanting and dancing.

[7] Jiva Gosvami was the most brilliant and influential of this school.

full God, not just an avatara of Visnu. While these men worked in Vrndavana, the holy place of Krsna and the Bhagavata, other devotees of Caitanya were writing religious lyrics and biographies, in the Bengali language, celebrating Caitanya as the living Krsna. During Caitanya's lifetime his Bengali followers were passionately devoted to him. But after his death no leader emerged with sufficient strength to hold the followers together, and there were serious splits in the movement.[8] Although the bhakti that Caitanya preached is far from dead in modern Bengal, there is now only a remnant of the former intense conviction that once existed.

Of Caitanya, a devotee (Bhaktivedanta 1968: Bookjacket) says:

> Many philosophers recognize God to be a force that is beyond name or form, but Caitanya Mahaprabhu taught that *God is a Person* [emphasis mine], who has Form, Qualities, Name and Pastimes—but Who is nevertheless Absolute and Transcendental and beyond anything we have experienced in this material world.
>
> Lord Caitanya journeyed up and down the subcontinent of India to deliver the easiest, most glorious method of self-realization: chanting of the Hare Krsna mantra. His explanations of the esoteric Vedanta Sutra converted many impersonalists, turning them from dried sticks into blooming flowers. He led thousands in massive kirtan parades of ecstasy, and even caused the tigers in the jungle to swoon.

According to Dimock (1966: 42), the uniqueness of the Bengali school is based in its emphasis upon four ideas: (1) Krsna's manifestation as a cowherd boy who frolics with the cowherd girls (gopis); (2) the contention that Krsna is the supreme deity, not just an incarnation of Visnu; (3) the description of religious experience in esthetic terms; and (4) a formalized sublimation of sexual and emotional erotic experience as a means of experiencing the divine. He (1966: 42) also considers the *Bhagavata Purana*[9] (called the *Srimad-Bhagavatam* by Bhaktivedanta Swami) to be the unifying link with all the other bhakti movements of India. It is this text that is the foundation of the Bengali movement's ideology and practice.

The *Bhagavatam*, which some scholars attribute to an anonymous author sometime during the ninth or tenth century A.D.,[10] can be regarded as a kind of New Testament of Vaisnavism and remains, especially in its Tenth Canto, the most popular of all Indian legends. The famed lilas (pastimes) of Krsna[11] from the Tenth Canto are so endlessly enacted, recited, and sung by children and youth that

---

[8] These splits, such as the one mentioned by Dimock (1966: 53) between Nityananda and Advaita, are ignored by Bhaktivedanta. In Appendix I the reader will see that Bhaktivedanta Swami claims both in his disciplic line.

[9] Radhakrishnan, an Indian philosopher, is of the opinion that Indian philosophy, in general, takes its "origin in life and enters back after passing through the schools. The great works of Indian philosophy do not have that 'ex cathedra' character which is so prominent a feature of the later criticisms and commentaries. The *Bhagavad-gita* and the *Upanisads* are not remote from popular belief. They are the great literature of the country, and at the same time vehicles of the great systems of thought. The *Puranas* contain the truth dressed up . . . to suit the weak understanding of the majority. The hard task of interesting the multitude in metaphysics is achieved in India" (McDermott 1970: 69). The *Bhagavata Purana* is also called the *Srimad-Bhagavatam* and *the Spotless Purana*.

[10] Taking his argument from the *Bhagavatam*, Bhaktivedanta Swami declares both that Vyasadeva wrote the *Bhagavatam* and that he did so at a much earlier date.

[11] Bhaktivedanta Swami has published a version of the Tenth Canto as *Krsna: The Supreme Personality of Godhead* and is constantly at work on translations of the other cantos. See Appendix II for a list of his works.

they have spread beyond the Vaisnava tradition throughout India. A main objective of the *Bhagavatam* is to illustrate, explain and promote devotion to Krsna. Bhakti (devotion) is not a new element; it always held a major place in the *Bhagavad-gita* where it was expressed primarily as meditation (concentration of thoughts on the deity). In the *Bhagavatam*, it becomes a passionate devotion of one's whole self in complete surrender to God, a total way of life that is the only way to true salvation. All traditional types of theological proofs and arguments are used by the Bengali movement's leading theologian, Jiva Gosvami (1961: 169), to prove the direct revelation of the *Bhagavatam*.

It is the text of the *Bhagavatam* that is central to the ideology of ISKCON, and its translation is considered by Bhaktivedanta Swami to be his major writing project and life work. Hopkins (1966: 11) points out that there is represented in the *Bhagavatam* an almost complete break with the traditional religious ceremonies based on the Vedas. He also notes the absence of qualifications based on birth and status that would ordinarily restrict participation in orthodox ceremonies. The *Bhagavatam* identifies the Vedas with the manifested Lord, and their authority is not denied. At points at which the Vedic teachings do not conflict with bhakti, there is no criticism. But at points where there is conflict, or where it is necessary to show the special value of devotion, the *Bhagavatam* shows no hesitation in demonstrating the weaknesses of orthodox Vedic religion. The basic criticism of the *Vedas* and orthodoxy is their ineffectiveness, especially in regard to the path of meditation. Krsna (Hopkins 1966: 12) says:

> Yoga does not bring me under control, nor Samkhya (a Vedic philosophical system), nor the recitation of the Veda to oneself, nor religious austerity, nor abandonment, nor the merit of sacrifices, nor a donation to a priest.
>
> I am overcome by bhakti alone;[12] I myself am the friend of good persons because of (their) faith; bhakti intent on me purifies even Svapakas (a low subcaste group) from (the sins of) their birth.

Significant differences between bhakti religion and Vedic orthodox religion are stressed by the *Bhagavatam*. Special emphasis is placed on the independence of bhakti from all other means of salvation and on the highest importance of devotional (bhakti) activity. This is the form of worship that is practiced by the Krsna Conscious movement and is set forth for the devotees by their spiritual master, Prabhupada. In his *Bhagavad-gita As It Is*, he attempts to resolve all conflicts that may arise in the reading of *Gitas* translated by other authors which may not be interpreted in the light of the *Srimad-Bhagavatam*.[13] As one devotee tells it:

> Personally I have had practical experience in trying to understand the *Bhagavad-gita* both alone and with a guru. . . I read the Gita twice and was very

[12] For a modern description of the emotional aspects of bhakti, see Tagore's (1952) masterpiece *Gitanjali*, a contemplative mystical masterpiece.

[13] Bhaktivedanta (1972a: Vol. I, 25) states, "The purpose of the *Vedas* and *Puranas* are one and the same. They want to ascertain the absolute truth." And (1972a: Vol. I, 1–2), "Being unaware of such significance of the *Bhagavatam*, the Indian mind has been used to hold that the *Bhagavatam* carries only the bhakti cult . . . and is not directly concerned with the teachings of the Vedas. . . It has therefore been the signal service of Sri Caitanya and his school of Gaudiya Vaisnavas to install the *Bhagavatam* in the place of honour which it deserves as the only rightful descendent of the Vedic lore coming down straight from the Bhagavan Vyasadeva himself."

interested, but somehow or other I could not understand the meaning of Krsna either as a person or a force. . . I feel safe in saying that the *Gita* would have always remained enigmatic to me had not the explanations of the spiritual master and the Hare Krsna mantra which he delivered to me opened that locked door. Actually we are all prisoners of conditioned life, and no amount of literature within the prison can free us. We can only be freed by someone from the outside. Then once freed we can read these great literatures in their true light.

The most salient feature of the *Bhagavatam* is the importance of devotional activity. This activity basically revolves around the worship of the forms and images[14] of God and consists of seeing, touching, worshipping, praising, cleaning, decorating, and making offerings to these images. Most of this devotional service is performed in temples. Great merit is attached to establishing temples, erecting images, and giving donations for the support of worship in temples. Much of the devotional activity is performed in groups. There are processions, festivals, and temple gatherings at which the devotees dance, chant, play musical instruments, and recite stories about the Lord. Besides participation in these festivities, they work together in and around the temple. The devotees must also follow high personal standards, a subject which will be discussed in the following chapter.

The religious and social teachings of the *Bhagavatam* have two purposes. The main purpose is to establish bhakti religion against any opposition. The major opposition, says Hopkins (1966: 18), "comes from persons committed to the defense of their traditional religious and social status" gained through the caste system. The secondary purpose is the recognition of those who have both the need and ability for salvation through devotion; for the *Bhagavatam* considers the poor and miserable as objects of compassion, rather than people reaping a just reward for past sins.

Hopkins (1966: 22) surmises:

> The movement was probably led by devoted ascetics whose learning and prestige gave the movement its structure. It drew its support from low caste social and economic groups that were despised by the rest of society, but their poverty and distress made them naturally sympathetic to a devotional religion based on faith and simplicity and led by persons who were themselves poor. The establishment of temples and the various group activities indicate that the movement was urban rather than rural and drew its support from the members of the depressed urban classes that would be present in sufficient numbers to give the movement stability.

With these considerations in mind, we will return to examine further details of the sociological context of the *Bhagavad-gita* and subsequent changes brought about by the *Srimad-Bhagavatam* which make this philosophy relevant to today's youth.

The *Bhagavad-gita* begins with Krsna addressing Arjuna on a battlefield; Arjuna is not a dedicated monk, but a warrior by birth and profession. In the *Gita* we find that the caste system is presented as a natural order. Men are divided into four

---

[14] A devotee, Gour Hari commented after reading this manuscript that the use of the word image is misleading because Krsna says that these deities are my form. This is not a symbol, it is Krsna! Gour Hari gave an example of a person wishing to mail a letter. If that person just puts the letter in any box it won't go anywhere; if he puts it in an official mailbox it goes directly to its destination. Similarly, if you worship a bona fide deity, not just an image, you are worshipping the personal form, called the arca-vigraha (deity incarnation). (See Chapter 3.)

groups[15] according to their capacities and characteristics; each group has its peculiar duties, ethics, and responsibilities, and these must be accepted. A man must go forward from his given position; he cannot leap forward. One must prefer to die doing his own duty, for the duty of another can bring him into great spiritual danger (Prabhavananda and Isherwood 1951: 39; Bhaktivedanta 1968: 76–77). These and other examples point to a religion in tune with a society that includes intellectuals, priests, warring factions, and a pastoral base for support. Scholars have presented a picture of an earlier society with a vigorous, confident culture which approached its gods joyously; later, at the time of the *Srimad-Bhagavatam*, it becomes characterized by a philosophical yearning for totality and a certainty of the unity of all things. It is also in a social sense a revolution of the poor and distressed. The *Bhagavatam* does not acknowledge the superiority of even Brahmanas simply on the basis of birth—it is those devoted to bhakti who are said to be the highest of men.[16]

The opening of devotional religion to the depressed urban classes can be seen as a parallel to the situation in which youth in the "betwixt and between" period feel society has failed them. They also wish to break out of society's prescribed roles and out of what they consider to be the coercive character of today's society. To the devotees of ISKCON, the choice of bhakti religion is the way out. Both the poor and distressed of Hopkins formulation and our alienated youth groups share the characteristics that Turner (1969: 125) lays out for liminal persons, those who often seem to be an "ill-assorted bunch of phenomena." Both groups: "(1) fall in the interstices of social structure, (2) are on its margins, or (3) occupy the lowest rungs." Caitanya swept through a large part of sixteenth-century India with his bhakti religion. Today Bhaktivedanta Swami, bringing Caitanya's message to modern youth, aims to sweep through twentieth-century America with as great a force as Caitanya's earlier movement. Like Caitanya, Bhaktivedanta Swami appeals to the emotions as well as the intellect, and is able to instill devotion in liminal persons. In his belief of direct disciplic succession, he seems to fill a role similar to that of Caitanya. Moreover, his devotees are convinced he is preaching the same message as this former incarnation of God. One devotee phrases it this way:

> My most humble obeisances to His Divine Grace Prabhupada, who appeared on this date just before the turn of the century in the family of a pure devotee. He has been charged, by the highest authority, with the responsibility of spreading this pure love of God to the western world, where the rampant diseases of impersonalism and voidism are the causes of so much spiritual confusion and are the roots of the soul killing civilization current here today. With His Divine

[15] The four Vedic castes are Brahmanas (priests), Kshatriyas (warriors), Vaishyas (merchants) and Sudras (servants, laborers).

[16] "Caitanya taught that one is brahmana by qualification, not by birth. In the Bhagavad-gita Krsna states, 'Peacefulness, self-control, austerity, purity, tolerance, honesty, wisdom, knowledge and religiousness—these are the qualities by which the brahmanas work.' Rupa Gosvami further cites the *Padma Purana* (another Puranic text): 'Everyone has the right to execute devotional service just as he has the right to take early bath. . . Lower caste people who are considered less than sudra are also initiated into the Vaisnava cult. . . They surpass the ordinary brahmanas.' Actually the Vaisnava, who is transcendental, is better than a brahmana, who may be conditioned to goodness. But we accept the proposal of Lord Caitanya; 'I am neither Hindu, nor brahmana, nor sannyasi (the renounced order), I am the servant of the servant of God.' " Giriraja dasa Brahmacari (*Back to Godhead*, No. 43, p. 22).

ning, the Dam of delusion was broken, and the western world is being
ith pure love of God—the same joyous inundation that first swept
ndia 500 years ago with the advent of Lord Caitanya Mahaprabhu, the
ciful of all incarnations.

KCON movement gains legitimacy and prestige through its claims to
roots in India, its body of Indian tradition, Vedic literature, use of the Sanskrit
language, and its spiritual master. Many youths find themselves attracted by the
exoticism of the ceremonies and proudly remind visitors to the temple that the *Gita*
is five thousand years old, older than the New Testament. Prayers are said in
Sanskrit, and whatever scripture has been learned in Sanskrit is proudly recited at
the least provocation.

THE GURU RETURNS TO INDIA

The Hare Krsna chanters first appeared in America in 1966. Americans were
shocked and amused to see devotees dressed in Indian dhotis and saris chanting in
Sanskrit, and regarded them as a novelty. In 1971, Bhaktivedanta Swami returned
to India from the West with his coterie of foreign personal servants and devotees.
Giriraja dasa Brahmacari (*Back to Godhead*, No. 43, p. 23) who accompanied the
guru on the trip to India reports:

> Now it is time for the Indians to be surprised. For the first time in many years,
> Indians in the downtown sectors of her major cities are seeing this same per-
> formance of sankirtana, as taught and popularized by Lord Caitanya, who
> advented himself in India 480 years ago. Yet instead of seeing Indians chanting
> as one would expect in India, the Indians are astonished to see that the chanters
> are actually Americans and Europeans, dressed in the traditional garb of Indian
> sadhus (holy men). These American and European devotees are following the
> Vedic system even more strictly than the Indians.

Some Indians are impressed by the determination and eagerness of the devotees,
although they regard them as curiosities, even as entertainment, and often as a
threat. Devotees who have visited India report much hostility to their presence
there and tell stories of the violence directed toward them by much of the
population.

The *Times of Delhi* (Saturday, November 13, 1971) reports an event in which
thirty American and European devotees of Bhaktivedanta appeared before a dais:

> . . . extravagantly decorated with strings of marigold flowers and mango leaves.
> White sheets were spread over the platform and a velvet sofa ornately designed
> for the leader of the movement. The swami's entry was quite dramatic. The
> chanting by the devotees reached a frenzy as he entered and they jumped and
> screamed for joy. Then, all of them lay prostrate in reverence to their spiritual
> leader.

The devotees say that when Prabhupada came to the United States, he told them,
"You are living in the greatest country in the world. If you take to this Krsna Consciousness movement, the whole world will follow your example." The devotees
believe that their guru has now brought Hare Krsna chanting back to India from
the West. They think that Indians are anxiously observing the example of the

West, desirous of becoming technologically and materially advanced, and are thereby forgetting God. The devotees tell the Indians that the West is disgusted with so-called material happiness and is now looking to India for spiritual guidance. They regard themselves as living proof for India that where money, sex, alcohol, divorce, coffee, cigarettes, washing machines, telephones, electric can openers, schools, poverty programs, hamburgers, milk shakes, T.V. dinners, hedonism, baseball and impersonalism have failed to bring happiness Krsna has succeeded. Now Krsna's pure devotee has returned to India to remind the people of their "blissful heritage." The devotees also believe misconceptions about Krsna to be rampant in India. However, these can be cleared up by reference to revealed scripture especially as their spiritual master tells it. Just as in America where there are so many Christians in name only, India has many Hindus who have accepted their religious tradition from their parents but who are not sincere believers in Krsna as presented by the disciplic succession according to the Vedas.

The belief held by the devotees, that one is brahmana by qualification and not by birth, has called forth criticism from some Indians. A letter in response to a *Times of Bombay* article (November 1970; quoted in *Back to Godhead*, No. 43, p. 17) states,

> As far as my knowledge goes, these foreign Hindus of the Hare Krsna movement cannot be equal to the native original brahmanas and Hindus.[17] They will have to be relegated to the lower castes. It is significant to see one of the newly converted sadhus, Sri Gopala dasa, formerly Charles Polan of Chicago, stated that he was a construction worker formerly. Doing Sudras' work, it would thus become necessary to allot the three lower castes to these foreign converts according to their profession.

Other Indians regard the disciples as a "sporadic fad of sentimentalists"; others comment, "Because you come from a rich country you can afford to spend your time chanting like this. When we become rich like you, we'll do this too." Still others say, "Yes, why don't you go back to your country and leave us alone? These philosophies have kept us back long enough. It is fine for you to chant, but what about the starving masses? It is hard enough to meditate on an empty stomach."

The devotees counter these criticisms by emphasizing that wherever they went in India they were favorably received by great crowds; moreover, what they are really emphasizing is pure love of God. One devotee (*Back to Godhead*, No. 43, p. 30) described their participation at a vedanta sadhu meeting in the town of Surat:

> When it was time for our program we simply looked at Srila Prabhupada and he said, "Begin chanting" and we did. . . Here the people are reaching to something that was lost to them and now returned to them. . . All over India they have been poisoned and have forgotten, and it is our task to bring them one-pointed purity. . . And then in the midst of our explosion of holy names, Prabhu-

---

[17] For a discussion of some of the peculiarities of Hinduism see Weber (1958: 8–9), especially where he points out, "One belongs to a strictly birth religion, like Hinduism, merely by being born to Hindu parents. However, Hinduism is 'exclusive' in the sense that in no other way can the individual enter its community, at least the circle of those considered fully qualified religiously. Hinduism does not wish to encompass mankind. No matter what his belief or way of life, anyone not born a Hindu remains an outsider, a barbarian to whom the sacred values of Hinduism are in principle denied." Compare this view to that of Bhaktivedanta and his devotees who aim for a worldwide ISKCON movement.

pada stood up and danced. The place was sur-charged with spiritual energy, and even hard westernized reporters cried in ecstasy.

The meetings went on the following day, but the devotees were requested not to come back. In the view of the devotees, their kirtana disrupted the verbose lectures of mental speculators who belabored one fine point after another, but never understood the spirit-soul as the devotees do. With a righteous indignation, the devotees shrugged off all opinions different from their own.

The guru's expressed purpose was to return India to the state of former God consciousness which he believed they had lost to material consciousness. Bhaktivedanta's return had all the earmarks of a triumph. The swami led his devoted following, who at every stop along the way prepared pagentry and a dramatic entrance for him. Rich trappings and American personal servants were a flamboyant part of the entourage. Although there was nothing new in the teachings of Bhaktivedanta (or any of the other returning gurus), they received much coverage in the Indian press because of the great publicity they were given in Europe and America. Recognition abroad leads to recognition at home, so "going foreign" has become very prestigious. And foreign devotees are an important status symbol, proving that the materialistic West is turning to spiritual India for guidance.

In addition, Bhaktivedanta has arranged for a grand style, opulent temple, school, and asrama (communal living quarters) to be constructed in Mayapur, India, designed to become the world center of the ISKCON movement. The cost of this temple will run into millions of dollars. The guru has already received a donation of approximately one million dollars from a wealthy Indian and will be raising more with his "book fund." The swami has called for many American devotees to come to India to supervise the building of this temple. Some have already left for India, and more will follow as soon as they are able to raise the three hundred dollars required for airfare. With this Mayapur temple serving as the world center of ISKCON and the 108 centers that the spiritual master has requested of the devotees around the world, there will remain a permanent personal tribute to him in his mother India even after his disappearance. Although Bhaktivedanta was told by his spiritual master to bring Krsna Consciousness to the English-speaking western world, he has decided to attempt to bring the philosophy to the entire world and also to return triumphantly to India.

4 / The concept of bhakti:

its meaning for devotees

I offer my humble obeisances unto His Divine Grace Prabhupada A. C. Bhaktivedanta Swami . . .
who opened the Bhagavad Gita and explained Sri Krsna's message verse by verse
and set his names—Hare Krsna, Hare Krsna, Krsna Krsna, Hare Hare, Hare
Rama, Hare Rama, Rama Rama, Hare Hare—on the lips of the young,
who, by contact only, warmed their hearts and lit the fires of love of God in their
souls and smeared their eyes with the ointment of devotion. (Hayagriva dasa
Adhikari)

Krsna Consciousness claims to be the revival of the original consciousness
of the living being—the conscious awareness that one is eternally related to God,
or Krsna. The true self (soul) is thought to be eternal, ever existent, but due to
the ignorance of material contamination, the soul is forced to assume a continuous
succession of material bodies. When one body dies, the soul immediately assumes
another body and is born again (samsara, transmigration of souls, round of
rebirths).[1] The individual forgets his past life and identifies with his present body,
which is for a devotee simply a temporary covering for the soul. This false identi-
fication with the temporary body must be overcome and a person must realize his
true position, namely that of the loving servant of Krsna. When he earns release
(mukti) from the cycle of birth, life, and death, he can resume his spiritual life
which is an eternal life of knowledge (jnana) and bliss (ananda) in the "loving
service of the supreme Lord."

This "loving service" is called bhakti and is considered to be the ultimate goal
of all religion, philosophy, and even life itself. Krsna himself is the "absolute
truth," and the function of the living entity is to live in "constant loving service to
the truth." Therefore, bhakti for the devotee is selfless dedication to Krsna by
which he is released from the power of maya (illusion) so that he can realize his
true relationship (rasa) with God. By giving pleasure to Krsna the devotee
experiences pleasure; but this return must not be the reason for the devotee's
desire to please Krsna. As Bhaktivedanta Swami states it (1968: 122):

A person acting in Krsna Consciousness is naturally free from the resultant
action of work. His activities are well performed for Krsna and therefore he does
not enjoy or suffer any of the effects of the work. . . Because everything is done
for Krsna, he enjoys only transcendental happiness in the discharge of this

[1] For this reason the devotees do not use the word die, but prefer to say disappear. Each
revered saint and sage has his appearance day which is often commemorated in some way.

service. Those who are engaged in this process are without desire for personal sense gratification.

Bhakti is the only means of gaining the right relationship with Krsna. The paths of work, ritual, and knowledge lead to lesser pleasures unless they are sanctified by bhakti. Bhakti is a state of active worship of the deity, not a state of inaction. The love and pleasure are reciprocal. Whatever the devotee gives to his Lord is returned with love many times over.

All living beings are believed to already be accepitng love from Krsna in the form of their food, material comforts, and in life itself. Krsna Consciousness is the process of becoming aware that all this is the gift of Krsna and of acting accordingly. All facilities and abilities at a devotee's disposal should be used in service to Krsna. In this way one's consciousness will be raised to the transcendental platform because he will be thinking of Krsna. Thus all senses and faculties can be engaged in the "transcendental" loving service of the Lord. It is not necessary to wait for death to enter the Kingdom of God, because one who is engaged in the transcendental loving service of the lord is living in the Kingdom of God (Krsna–loka), even before death. A devotee says, "He may still be on this earth, but because he is constantly serving Krsna, by the grace of Krsna he is constantly aware of Krsna everywhere."

The devotees say that one cannot create his own God and then claim to be constantly aware of God. Krsna is a distinct individual with distinct characteristics. They use the example that if someone wants to meet the president of the United States, he cannot create a fictional president and then claim to know the president of the United States. The president is a specific person with his specific form and characteristics, and unless one knows that specific person he cannot claim to know the president. Similarly, unless one knows the specific form and personality of Krsna, he cannot claim to know Krsna just because he has created some fictional God in his mind. In order to reach or to know Krsna, one must follow the instructions of Krsna, and these instructions are given in the scriptures.

The prime instruction is that one must revive his dormant love for Krsna. In the present age, known as the Kali-yuga, the recommended method for reviving this dormant love for Krsna is the process of constantly chanting the holy names of Krsna. This was revealed by Sri Krsna Caitanya, who said that in this age the easiest means of spiritual realization is the chanting of the holy names. Therefore, the ISKCON groups are dedicated to spreading the chanting of these holy names. The holy names were given to the devotees in an easily learned and repeated form known as the Mahamantra or great chanting by Caitanya. The Mahamantra is:

> Hare Krsna Hare Krsna,
> Krsna Krsna Hare Hare,
> Hare Rama Hare Rama,
> Rama Rama Hare Hare.

Hare means the supreme pleasure potency of the Lord.[2] Krsna is the original name of the Lord, and it means all-attractive. Rama is another name of the Lord meaning the enjoyer, because Krsna is the supreme enjoyer; the function of living

[2] The writer is aware that Hare may also have other meanings, but the devotees impute this meaning as official, so it is used here.

is thought to be for the enjoyment of Krsna. The devotees think that people are under the false impression that they are the enjoyers, while they are actually suffering in material existence. The living being cannot enjoy independently because living entities are always trying to accomplish the impossible. For this reason they are always frustrated. Their limited senses do not have the capacity for independent enjoyment, but when they use their senses to please the senses of Krsna, then they can be automatically satisfied. In doing so the senses of the individual become dovetailed with the supreme senses of Krsna, and the living being attains the pleasure and happiness that is otherwise impossible to find.

Bhakti is a state of active love for the deity, a seeking of that which is most beautiful and satisfying. Phenomenal earthly love can never be fully satisfying because it is transitory and imperfect. (Such active love is satisfying to God, but there could be no love like this if the lover and the beloved were the same. So dualism is stressed: God and men are held to be separate entities.) There are two types of bhaktas (practitioners of bhakti): those who are immediately able to cast off the bonds of maya and realize their natural state of intimate relationship with Krsna, and those who need to be led to the path of bhakti. The majority of the population fall into the second category. That is why most individuals are in the clutches of maya and are in need of assistance to extricate themselves from it. The spiritual master helps the would-be devotee through the preliminary stages to the point of pure love for Krsna.

The preliminary aspects of bhakti are:

1. Recognizing Krsna as one's only refuge.
2. Service to a spiritual master (guru).
3. Reading and listening to the *Bhagavad-gita* and the *Srimad-Bhagavatam*, Krsna's pastimes, and the writings of the guru.
4. Sankirtana, singing the names and praises of Krsna; this is the most powerful means of bringing about an attitude proper for bhakti and should be universally adopted in the present age of Kali.
5. Thinking constantly of the name, form, and pastimes of Krsna.
6. Serving the feet of the deities, seeing, touching, and worshipping the deities.
7. Performing rites and ceremonies learned from the guru, such as putting Vaisnava signs on one's body, taking the remains of an offering to the deity as prasada, drinking the water used to wash the deity, and so on.
8. Prostrating before the deity forms and the spiritual master.

These eight acts are meant to bring about the proper feeling of humility and self-surrender essential to bhakti. When one is completely surrendered, he is prepared to realize his true relationship to Krsna. As a brahmacari tells it,

These things are done out of regulation in the preliminary stages, but the goal is the spontaneous performance of these aspects of bhakti—just as when you begin to know somebody well you do things for him spontaneously in friendship. The goal is spontaneous love of God. This is a pure devotee.

The characteristics of a pure devotee are given in the *Bhagavad-gita* (Bhaktivedanta Swami 1968: 212–213) where the spiritual master writes in a purport:

Pure devotees, whose characteristics are mentioned here, engage themselves fully in the transcendental loving service of the lord. Their minds cannot be diverted from the lotus feet of Krsna. Their talks are solely transcendental. Twenty-four hours daily, they glorify the pastimes of the Supreme Lord. Their hearts and souls constantly submerged in Krsna, they take pleasure in discussing Him with other devotees. In the preliminary stage of devotional service they relish transcendental pleasure from the service itself; and in the later mature stage they are situated in the love of God and can relish the highest perfection which is exhibited by the Lord in his abode.

Bhakti is expressed by a devotee as,

. . . my pure eternal engagement. The practical thing is being engaged. The engagement should be service. We learn what the service is through the spiritual master. Sometimes it is difficult to perform what I know is the best spiritual service for my guru. One must use his intelligence to figure out the best thing. For instance, right now I could chant in the temple, read scriptures, write an article for *Back to Godhead* magazine or preach to a guest.

About bhakti a brahmacari says,

Doing what you are supposed to do, that is devotional service. It is nice to watch a pot cooking or drive a truck for Krsna. Devotional service is nice. Sometimes you can't do it because you eat too much—like refrgerator freaks. Eating too much gets you into heavy maya. Like after a feast there is Monday morning maya, but you chant your rounds and you can get rid of the maya. You make a vow to rid yourself of maya—you have been in maya so many times.

Yet another devotee feels that "by engaging in bhakti you immediately transcend. We are on the pure platform, but don't think you are pure. By staying on this platform you'll become pure. When we are pure the result is pure love—prema and bliss."

Bhakti is thought to be the way to pure love, and the individual should also experience bliss emanating from this feeling of love. Materialistic activities cannot bring pleasure, but the bhaktas experience such bliss that they easily relinquish all other pleasures. How can anybody be happy without Krsna?

Suppose, says the spiritual master, one is thrown into the ocean? How can he be happy there? That is not for us. One may be a very good swimmer, but how long will one be able to swim? He eventually becomes tired and drowns. Similarly, we are spiritual by nature—how can we be happy in this material world? It is not possible. But men are trying to remain here, making so many temporary adjustments for survival. This patchwork is not happiness. If one really wants happiness, he must attain love of Godhead. Unless one can love Krsna, unless one finishes with love for cats, dogs, country, nation and society and instead concentrates his love on Krsna, there is no question of happiness.

The guru tells his devotees that God is as real as we are, although we are under illusion. We are living as if this body were our factual self, although it is only a temporary manifestation. Lord Krsna and his abode, Krsna–loka, exist; one can go there, reach him, and associate with him. Spiritual life means to be in association with the Supreme Lord and to exist in bliss and knowledge eternally. Eternal association means to play with Krsna, to dance with and to love Krsna in many ways. As a passive devotee, when he considers Krsna as the supreme deity a worshipper feels awe, humbleness, and insignificance. As a servant, he feels as toward his master—respect, subservience, dedication. He feels the love of a friend for a friend, and the love of a parent and brother toward Krsna. As a lover he feels the highest and most intimate emotion of love, of lover for the beloved.

It is the manifestation of Krsna as the dark, two-armed[3] cowherd boy of the Srimad Bhagavatam that is fully real to the devotee, although Krsna is, of course, eternal and has manifested himself on earth in many ways and at many times. The stories of the *Bhagavatam* that deal with the pastimes of Krsna are filled with people who have various eternal relationships and degrees of intimacy with Krsna. There are his family, friends, and, closest of all, the gopis (cowherd girls) with whom Krsna engaged in love play. The bhakta should assume a relationship to Krsna that is suitable to himself, and through this relationship experience the love relationships that the people of the *Bhagavatam* feel toward Krsna.

Bhaktivedanta Swami gives an example of devotees who have the inclination to actually give service.

> They think, "Krsna wants to sit down. I will arrange a place for him. Krsna wants to eat. I will get him some nice food." And they actually make these arrangements. Other devotees play with Krsna as friends on equal terms. They do not know that Krsna is God; to them, Krsna is their lovable friend, and they cannot forget him for a moment. All day and all night, they think of Krsna. At night when they are sleeping they think, "Oh, in the morning I shall go and play with Krsna." And in the morning they go to Krsna's house and stand by while Krsna is decorated by his mother before going out to play with his friends in the fields. There is no other activity in Krsna–loka. There is no industry, no rushing to the office or any such nonsense. There is sufficient milk and butter, and everyone eats plentifully. Krsna is very fond of his friends, and sometimes he enjoys stealing butter for them. One can actually live this way, and that is the perfection of existence. We should hanker for that perfectional stage of life. Krsna Consciousness is the process to attain it.

Although spiritual life is considered to be blissful, it is not to be thought of as whimsical. In order to follow the regulative principles of bhakti-yoga as defined by the spiritual master and the authorized scriptures and to purify himself enough to reach the joyful spiritual platform, the prospective devotee joins an ISKCON temple.

THE TEMPLE

The Boston temple is a large bright blue, seventy-year-old wood frame building, which formerly served as a funeral home.[4] It overlooks a main street in a shabby section of the city populated by working class people and students. The temple consists of a basement and three floors, all of which are used intensively. The basement contains storage space, the incense business, the furnace, a washing machine, and has room for odd chores. The first floor includes an entrance hall, the dining room, an office for the president and temple commander, the tulasi tree cultivation room (this room is equipped with special plant lights and humidifying devices), the kitchen, and a small deity room. On the second floor is the temple room, a sewing room, a men's bathroom, a women's bathroom, a small business office, and two rooms which serve any necessary purpose during the day and are used for

[3] Krsna and other Indian deities have two- and four-armed forms. Sometimes they are even pictured with six arms.

[4] The Boston temple relocated and is now in an elegant brownstone building close to the Public Garden.

*Cleaning the entrance
to the temple.*

sleeping rooms at night. Separate sleeping rooms for male and female ISKCON members are on the third floor.

Most temples follow this general pattern. A large temple room, housing the deities, is always the dominating feature and the center of activity in each temple. The temple room is always as opulent as the devotees are able to make it. In contrast the rest of the rooms seem austere as they are completely devoid of furniture with the exception of an occasional desk or chair. The devotees quickly become accustomed to sitting cross-legged on the floor, eating from paper plates, and sleeping on the bare floors in a sleeping bag or on a quilt. During the day all sleeping bags and blankets are neatly put away so that the temple appears quite empty. At night any and all rooms can be used for sleeping.

Although the devotees believe that Krsna, the Supreme Lord, does not need an opulent temple, they say they take pleasure in worshipping the Lord in an opulent manner and keeping the temple clean. The Lord is not in need of big temples, and the pure devotee does not need an opulent setting in which to worship. Pure devotees who have the Lord in their hearts are prepared to live anywhere and to sleep under a tree if Krsna desires. The temple is meant not for the Lord or the devotees, but for people in general. The spiritual master (Bhaktivedanta 1972b: 160–1) has said,

Attention engaged in the service of the Lord, especially in dressing and decorating the temple, accompanied by musical kirtana and spiritual instructions from the scriptures, can alone save the common man from the hellish cinemas and the rubbish sex songs broadcast everywhere by radios. If one is unable to maintain a temple at home, he should go to a temple where ceremonies are regularly executed. Visiting the temple and looking at the profusely decorated forms of the Lord, well-dressed and in a well-decorated sanctified temple, naturally infuses the mundane mind with spiritual inspiration. People should visit holy places where temples and worship of the deities are specifically maintained. Formerly all rich men like kings and rich merchants constructed such temples under the direction of expert devotees of the Lord, like the six Gosvamins, and it is the duty of the common man to take advantage of these temples and festivals.

"The temple itself is not located in the mundane world," the devotees tell us. "This temple is not in Boston and that temple is not in New York. They are in Vaikuntha" (the spiritual planets). The devotees say they like to gather in the temple which, because everything is done in a manner conducive to Krsna Consciousness, is an entirely transcendental place. The spiritual master has stated that if one simply visits a temple, although not understanding the spiritual nature of the form of God in the deity, but merely appreciating the beautiful setting of the altar, that person will automatically become a devotee because of his appreciation of Krsna.

The colorful and luxurious temple room is dominated by a lavish altar which consists of three white marble steps leading up to a white marble stage-like platform backed by pink and white tiles. In the center of the platform are two realistic twenty-four-inch statues representing Krsna playing the flute beside his chief consort, Radharani (Radha). To the right are three wooden Jagannatha deities, resembling expressionistic African masks. Also on the right is a painting of Lord Caitanya and his disciples and pictures of the disciplic succession with prominence given to the picture of Bhaktivedanta Swami. The statues are gorgeously dressed in satin and lace, heavily bejewelled, and decorated with fresh flower garlands and bouquets. Silver articles used in the aratrika ceremony are placed to the extreme left side of the altar.

At the opposite end of the temple, facing the altar, is the red velvet vyasasana (the spiritual master's chair) with a pair of the spiritual master's shoes placed in front of it. At times Bhaktivedanta Swami's sweater or other articles of clothing are neatly folded and placed on the vyasasana. A picture of Bhaktivedanta Swami is usually placed on the vyasasana, showing a deeply lined face with a broad nose and thick jowls. The entire floor is covered with gleaming white tiles, the walls are painted lemon yellow, the windows are draped in bright pink, and everything is trimmed in gold, purple, blue, green, and white. The air is heavy with the scent of incense, and the total effect is a glistening piece of high psychedelia dazzling to behold.

THE DAILY ROUND

At 3:30 A.M. the brahmacaris are awakened by the chanting of Hare Krsna and brought to their feet. These early morning hours, the brahma-muhurta, are considered particularly auspicious for spiritual advancement (actually one hour and thirty-six minutes before sunrise is the most auspicious hour of the day), so devotees are required to awaken for the mangala-aratrika (the first aratrika of the day) ceremony and catch up on lost sleep later if necessary. Some especially fervent souls arise earlier, such as the pujari (the caretaker of the deities), who may be up as early as 3:00 A.M. doing her duties. At 3:30 A.M. the cooks begin preparing foods (prasada) which will be offered to the deities in the temple at the 5:00 A.M. aratrika ceremony. Also at 4:00 A.M. the girls start making flower garlands for the deities. Several days each week the temple vehicle departs early in the morning for the purchase of flowers, because only fresh flowers, preferably with a scent, are offered to the deities.

At the 5:00 A.M. aratrika, the Supreme Lord is greeted in the form of his deity incarnation, and every devotee is required to attend this aratrika. During the entire ceremony, the congregation chants the mahamantra (great mantra) said to be the heart and soul of Krsna Consciousness,[5] and sings the praises of Krsna and the guru. The deity form of the Lord is then fed (the feeding is performed through the offering and leaving of the prasada to the deity incarnations). At 6:00 A.M. everyone reassembles in the temple for the *Nectar of Devotion* and *Srimad-Bhagavatam* classes. Breakfast prasada is served at 8:45 A.M. Before and after breakfast each member of the temple cleans, does other temple-related work, and, if there are any spare moments, chants with japa beads. The beads are held while chanting Hare Krsna. During the rest of the day the devotees attend to their various duties such as printing press duties, making incense, speaking engagements, sewing, painting, cooking, deity care, bookkeeping, and construction tasks around the temple. At 11:00 A.M. the sankirtana party usually leaves in the temple van with the paraphernalia for the day's chanting. The devotees chant throughout the day in the parks and streets of the city where they happen to be and often go to chant at great distances from the temple. During sankirtana, the *Back to Godhead* magazines are distributed and/or peddled, and the brahmacaris beg for whatever donations they can get.

At 12:00 noon the food is again prepared and offered, and at 1:45 P.M. prasada is again taken. After prasada more devotees may go out on sankirtana. If the devotees are too far from the temple to return for prasada or wish to stay out longer, they will bring their food with them into the field. Chanting and distributing literature continues until 6:00 P.M., when the members return to the temple. Later they may take milk prasada, which may be warm, sweetened milk with cookies or cake, and still later, the devotees attend a 7:00 P.M. aratrika (sunda aratrika). Following the aratrika ceremony is the *Bhagavad-gita* class during which devotees and guests may ask questions which are answered on the authority of the spiritual master. By 10:00 P.M., all of the devotees "take rest" and the day is ended.

It is important to note that the rigid adherence to the bhakti schedule is recommended for all devotees. According to their duties and the depth of their dedication, the devotees will adhere to a strict schedule, since the practice of bhakti-yoga requires a strictly regulated life. There are those who oversleep and those whose busy schedules do not permit them to attend the two aratrika ceremonies required of each devotee daily. The more seasoned devotees are gentle with these new-

---

[5] When a friend from the karmi world, lost in sense gratification, asked a devotee how he could stand the austerity of temple life, the response was an incredulous, "Austerity! Who else dances before the Lord at 4 o'clock in the morning?"

comers who have trouble adjusting to their new and grueling schedules; however, after an adjustment period, a devotee is expected to conform to the temple schedule. If he does not, the temple president will speak to him requesting his conformance to the rules and regulations. Pressure will also be brought to bear by the other devotees who will urge him to be more disciplined and to perform his duties for Krsna.

The daily schedule[6] will conform to the standards described above for the daily round, but will, as a practical matter, vary in detail. The variety will be individual according to the demands on a devotee and will also be changed from time to time by the temple president to conform to seasonal sunrise hours or to meet scheduling demands. For instance, the meal hours at the Boston temple have been changed four times in the last year. Mainly the variations are only in small details such as these. The basic essentials of worship are always strictly observed as closely as possible. Each member is supposed to attend as many scripture classes as he can. For a short period attendance was taken, but this was discontinued due to the objections of the devotees.

Following are three daily schedules. The first is that of the pujari (the caretaker of the deities). "The worship schedule revolves around the deities' day," says the pujari, "and the temple activities are planned to revolve around this schedule, the observance of which is to be adhered to very strictly and conscientiously." The second is the daily schedule of the temple treasurer, who is less directly concerned with the transcendental aspects of worship and has a very practical job to do. The third is the schedule of an ISKCON press worker, who spends most of his daily waking hours participating in the printing of the spiritual master's books. All of the devotees observe the same schedule every day including Sunday. On Sunday, in addition to the regular duties, each member participates in the preparation of the temple and the feast for the guests who will be coming in the late afternoon. A feast is served and guests are urged to participate in the religious services that take place.

Pujari's Schedule

A.M.

3:30   Rise and shower; set everything in place for mangala-aratrika

4:00   Chant japa (prayer beads)

4:30   Wake up deities by ringing a bell; say mantras; take the deities out of their beds and put on their capes and crowns; set up and check to see that everything is prepared for the aratrika

4:45   Offer three trays of prasada, one for each section of the altar: Disciplic succession—Prabhupada, Caitanya, Saraswati; Radha and Krsna; and the Lord Jagannatha deities. The trays are left for fifteen minutes for the deities to "eat" their fill before they are removed.

5:00   Mangala-aratrika

5:30   Clean the altar

5:50   Get water for the deities' baths and get fresh clothes ready for the deities

---

[6] See Appendix III for the schedule of the New York City temple. Most temples follow a similar schedule with this as a prototype.

Preparing for the Sunday feast.

6:10 Bathe and dress the deities during the *Nectar of Devotion* and *Srimad-Bhagavatam* classes

7:15 Open curtains; play tape of Srila Prabhupada; go downstairs to clean up all the articles used in bathing and dressing the deities, such as their wash-cloths and towels, hang up their pajamas, and so on

7:45 Set up the next aratrika; chant for two minutes

8:00 Go to the kitchen to get the breakfast prasada trays for offering, and aesthetically arrange them

8:15 Put food trays for the deities on the altar

8:30 Dhoop aratrika

8:45 Take prasada herself with the other devotees

9:15 Chant japa in the temple

10:00 Circumambulate the temple

10:15 Go to the office to see if there is any business to do there

10:30 Clean the sewing room

11:00 Sew deities' clothes with the other women

11:20 Check the altar to see if everything is ready for the next aratrika; shower

11:40 Set up lunch trays

P.M.

12:00 Offer prasada

12:15 Chant or sew in the temple

1:00	Bnog aratrika
1:30	Deities rest—take off their jewelry and crowns and put them into bed (As much quiet as possible is maintained in the temple while the deities rest so that they will not be disturbed.)
1:45	Take prasada
2:15	Go out on sankirtana or have deity watch in the temple
3:30	Set up aratrika equipment; shower
3:50	Wake deities—put on their crowns and jewels
4:00	Offering prasada
4:15	Dhoop aratrika
4:30	Change deities' clothing; set up next aratrika
6:00	Talk to the deities about what she has done that day or what she should have done and didn't do; chant rounds or read *Srimad-Bhagavatam*
6:30	Hang up deities' clothes; shower; go to kitchen to arrange trays for the deities
7:00	Offer prasada; Tulasi Devi worship in which all devotees should participate
7:15	Sunda aratrika
7:45	*Bhagavad-gita* class; clean aratrika articles and set them up again for the next aratrika
8:30	Teaching of Lord Caitanya reading
8:45	Offering to the deities
9:00	Aratrika
9:15	Devotees take milk prasada
9:30	Deities put to rest
10:10	Hang up the deities' clothes; read a few minutes in scripture
10:30	Take rest

Temple Treasurer's Work Schedule

A.M.

3:30	Rise and shower
4:15	Aratrika
5:00	Chant japa
5:30	*Srimad-Bhagavatam* reading
6:00	Chant japa
7:00	Treasury work
7:30	Tulasi worship
7:45	Prasada
8:00	Clean silver; do requisitions
9:00	Class
10:00	Treasury; chant japa

P.M.

12:30	Lunch prasada
1:15	Sankirtana

5:00   Shower and prasada
5:30   Reading time
6:00   Treasury work
6:30   *Bhagavad-gita* class
7:00   Treasury work; answer phone calls, visit with potential members
9:30   Rest

Press Worker's Schedule

A.M.
4:00   Rise
4:15   Aratrika and class
5:30   Chant
6:00   Rest
7:30   Prasada
8:00   Work; clean-up
10:50 Sankirtana
11:30 Prasada

P.M.
12:15 Work at the press
5:00   Prasada
5:30   Work at the press
6:30   *Nectar of Devotion* class
7:00   Chant japa
8:00   *Bhagavad-gita* class
8:30   Work at the press
10:00 Rest

GREETING THE LORD: THE ARATRIKA CEREMONY

Many devotees feel that visitors to the temple rarely understand that they are experiencing an ancient ritual which is believed to be over five thousand years old. Visitors who attribute little or no significance to the chanting of the holy names may find the chanting loud and repetitious. The Supreme Lord who is present in the deity form is considered to be the proprietor of the temple. The deities are not idols. They are incarnations of Krsna appearing in material elements. This is explained by Bhaktivedanta Swami (1969: 30):

The Lord appears in the form of Arca, or deities supposedly made of earth or stone. These forms, engraved from wood or stone or any other matter, are not idols, however, as is held by the iconoclasts. In the present state of our imperfect material existence, we cannot see the Supreme Lord on account of our imperfect vision. . . This does not mean that such devotees, who are in the lowest stages of devotional service, are worshipping an idol. In fact, they are worshipping the Lord, who has agreed to appear before them in a particular way which is approachable by them. . . Because he is full of inconceivable potencies, God can

The aratrika ceremony: greeting the Lord.

accept our service through any sort of medium, and He can convert His different potencies according to His own will.

It is held, therefore, that because we cannot see God with our present senses, he may choose to appear in this material world in a form composed of material elements. Since he is the controller of both the material and spiritual energies, when he appears in such a form it is no longer considered material. So God has agreed to appear before the neophyte devotees in the deity form so they may worship him, feed him, and dress him. The forms of the Lord are manifested in his incarnations as Jagannatha or Radha-Krsna deities. Anyone who is sincerely looking for spiritual union with the Supreme Lord will not refuse to worship his authorized forms (the authority is the Vedic literature and the disciplic succession). Deity worship is especially recommended by Prabhupada for those entangled in the material complications of family life and for neophyte devotees because it will help them purify their existence and make progress in spiritual knowledge. A male devotee points out that it is his belief that, "If you treat a deity like an idol it will remain an idol to you forever, but if you treat it as Krsna himself it will sing and dance for you. So I say to the deities, 'Krsna I am rotten—I am fallen—please accept this offering.' "

The deities are regularly worshipped by an ancient ceremony called an aratrika which ideally is performed six times each day, although in smaller temples it may be performed only four times daily. The purpose of greeting the Lord is simply that Krsna likes it. Prabhupada says that all things are offered to Krsna because he likes and enjoys them, A leader begins by chanting a Sanskrit prayer, and the devotees join in responsively, accompanied by the rhythmic jangle of karatals (finger cymbals), the beat of the mrdangas, and chords from a small harmonium. During the entire ritual the mahamantra is chanted and the "prabhupada step" (a simple one-two step) is danced. At first the chanting is soft, but grows steadily louder, the mrdanga beat more insistent, until the devotees are jumping up and down, arms raised high and bare feet thumping against the floor with the rhythm. A few devotees seem particularly ecstatic with their eyeballs rolled up, moving in what appears to be an epileptic frenzy with their arms akimbo like the many-limbed Lord Shiva.

When the aratrika ceremony is about to begin, three silver prasada trays are brought up to the temple from the kitchen where they have been attractively arranged by the pujari. Water is sprinkled on the place where each tray will be laid to purify the spot.[7] The trays, brought into the temple covered because the food must never be seen until offered, are placed on the altar. The curtain is closed, the covers removed, and the pujari goes outside the curtains where she rings a small silver bell and says prayers offering the food to Prabhupada. The food cannot be offered directly to Krsna because Krsna is great and "we are very, very small," says the pujari, "just as a menial laborer in a factory cannot approach the president directly." The food is left for the deities "to eat" for fifteen minutes and at noon for one hour. When the deities have finished eating, the pujari steps behind the curtain to make certain everything is all right, rings the bell again, opens the curtain, and the elaborate ceremony begins.

The pujari begins the ritual by standing to the right side of the altar where all the necessary articles are placed in readiness on a silver tray. Here she whispers her prayers. She washes her right hand with water from a silver goblet, then sprinkles three drops of water on some incense (each item to be offered is first sprinkled with three drops of water to purify it), picks up three sticks of incense, lights them with a candle, and begins to wave the incense in front of the pictures of the disciplic succession with seven circular motions of her right arm, ringing a bell held in her left hand throughout the entire ceremony. Next she moves to the center, repeats the procedure in front of Radha and Krsna, and then moves on to the right section of the altar to make the offering to the Jagannatha deities. After the deities' incense offering is completed, the pujari walks backward to the left-hand corner, while offering the incense to the devotees. Two incense sticks are placed in the incense burner, and the third is used to light a camphor lamp. Then the incense stick is placed with the others in the incense holder. The offering is repeated exactly the same way with the camphor lamp, which is handed to a waiting devotee who walks with it through the assembled devotees. Each devotee passes his hand over the flame and touches the hand to his forehead as a sign of respect. This procedure is repeated for the third item to be offered, a ghee lamp with five wicks, which is also passed through the assembled devotees in the same way as the camphor lamp after the offering. The fourth offering is some water from a small conch shell. Some of

[7] Water is never taken out of the bathroom, but from the kitchen which should be as clean as the temple at all times.

the water is poured into a small silver bowl and then offered; for each offering a little more water is poured into the bowl. At the end of the offering, all the remaining water is poured into the bowl and the shell is returned to its brass stand. The fifth offering is a handkerchief, the sixth a flower, the seventh a fan of peacock feathers, and the eighth and last item is a yak tail (camara) on a silver handle.

At the close of the ceremony the pujari blows a large conch shell, a symbolic sounding of Krsna's flute, and all the devotees stop chanting and lie flat on the floor. The pujari then says responsive prayers, naming names of Krsna and his pure devotees and purifying them. The assembled devotees repeat each prayer and end each shouting "jaya" (spiritual victory). The silver bowl containing the offered water from the conch shell is then taken by a devotee through the congregation, and a drop or two is sprinkled on everyone's head. The plates are removed from the altar and brought to the kitchen where the food is transferred to plates to be served to the devotees at prasada time.

When the ceremony is completed, the altar is cleaned and dried, and the floor is mopped. As in all temple activities, much emphasis is placed on cleanliness and purification. All articles are washed, polished, and placed back on the altar, clean for each ceremony (see pujari's schedule). One pujari is in charge of caring for the temple deities as his or her special duty, and this person assumes the responsibility for keeping the altar and the equipment in order. Since there are six aratrikas daily, some of these ceremonies are assigned to other devotees who qualify to perform them after having undergone the brahmana thread ceremony.

In the daily temple worship, bouquets and garlands of fresh flowers are offered to the Jagannatha and Radha-Krsna deities. After these garlands have been worn by the deities, they are distributed to the various devotees to wear and are considered very auspicious. Anyone who puts a flower garland that has been formerly used by Krsna in his deity form around his neck, becomes relieved of all disease and reactions to sinful activities, and gradually becomes liberated from the contamination of matter.

TULASI DEVI WORSHIP

At the end of two aratrika ceremonies each day, usually in morning and evening, is a special ceremony for the sacred plant, Tulasi Devi. This plant is worshipped as Krsna's pure devotee. The devotees consider Tulasi Devi to be a spirit-soul in the body of a plant because it is possible for a spirit-soul to appear in plant form as well as human and animal form. Further, it is said that Krsna is very fond of tulasi leaves and buds. By offering obeisances to this plant, the devotees believe, volumes of sinful activities can immediately be vanquished. Simply by seeing, touching, or eating the leaves of this plant, one can be relieved of all distresses and diseases. If one sows a tulasi tree somewhere, he will become devoted to Krsna. It is also said that every Hindu in India, not just Vaisnavas, takes special care of the tulasi tree. Each day the plant is brought into the temple. It is placed upon an elaborately decorated stand while the devotees circumambulate, chanting and dancing with their eyes fixed upon it. During the entire tulasi worship ceremony, a small bell is rung by the devotee who cares for the plant.

Tulasi Devi worship.

A devotee in each temple is assigned the care of the tulasi plants, and a special room is set aside for their cultivation. The room is equipped with a special fluorescent plant light and humidifier. Because the tulasi's growth and development is believed to be a barometer of the temple devotees' love and devotion to Krsna, particular care is taken to give the plant love and devotion. The Boston temple has found tulasi trees difficult to grow, but has finally met with some success. Advice is constantly sought regarding the cultivation of this plant. Recently a swami, who has enjoyed some success with his plants, suggested that the devotees try his method —offering some real jewels (a cat's eye and pearls) by putting them on the soil of the plant. He also suggested they add more sand to the soil. In all conversation, Tulasi Devi is referred to by name or by the pronoun "she," because she is considered to be a fully conscious being.

JHULANA-YATRA: THE SWING CEREMONY

Jhulana-yatra, the swing ceremony, takes place occasionally at a special service and feast for guests at the temple. Each person present takes a turn pushing the deities in a swing. Through this activity, a person is actively involved in service to the deities which ideally should plant the seed of love for the deities in his heart. Any additional devotional service should foster this love.

An elaborate, cage-like, pink-satin swing decorated with pink satin ruffles, jewels,

Jhulana-yatra: the swing ceremony.

and flowers is brought into the temple and attached to hooks on the ceiling in front of the vyasasana. While the devotees and guests are chanting, the pujari carries the deities up to the swing, places them inside, and fastens them into the swing. The president of the temple stands at the right side of the swing in a prayerful position with his palms pressed together and held in front of his chin. At the front left corner stands another devotee, waving incense sticks throughout the entire ceremony. Also standing on the right side where the people are lined up to push the deities is a female devotee with a small brass pitcher of water; as each person gets ready to push the swing, she pours a drop or two of water into the person's hands to purify them. The pujari begins the ceremony by gently pushing the swing. She then steps to the right of the swing and stands in a prayerful position with her eyes fixed on the deities, smiling all the while. Each person takes a turn pushing the swing. On the second or third round, a devotee holding a basket of flowers appears. Each person, after receiving the water on his hands, picks up some flower petals and places them around the deities before he pushes the swing. After a person pushes the swing, he joins the rest of the group circumambulating the swing and chanting. The ceremony continues until the incense sticks are burned low. The deities are then removed from the swing and returned to the altar by the pujari, and the swing is removed by two brahmacaris.

THE CALENDRICAL ROUND

Occasions for the remembrance of Krsna are ekadasi days (fast days) which come "twice a month on the eleventh day of the moon, both waning and waxing" (Bhaktivedanta 1970: 214). On that day, according to Vedic regulations, the devotees should chant all day and night and observe twenty-four hours of fasting.

In the temples visited, the devotees chant more than the usual rounds of japa beads, sleep less, take less care of themselves, and observe a partial fast. They abstain from grains and beans.

There are three other fast days in which total twenty-four hour fasting is observed. The most important of these is Janmastami, Krsna's appearance day. "This Janmastami day is the most opulent festival day for the devotees and it is still observed with great pomp in every Hindu house in India. Sometimes even the devotees of other religious groups take advantage of this auspicious day and enjoy the performance of the ceremony of Janmastami," says Prabhupada.

There are many more annual occasions which are always observed by Vaisnavas in India; but in Krsna Consciousness the temple president can decide whether to observe one or all of these holidays according to what he considers the needs of his particular temple. In San Francisco and in London the devotees chose to observe the Rathayatra Festival, which is also called the Lord Jagannatha cart festival. Carts were constructed by the devotees to carry the Lord Jagannatha deities: Krsna, his brother Balarama, and his sister Subhadra. Then they were wheeled through the city of San Francisco to the beach. Those who participated in this event chanted, danced, ate prasada, and joined the procession following the carts. The Rathayatra procession, with its gigantic, extravagantly decorated deity carts is meant to attract materialistic people. Said a devotee, "Rathayatra is a love festival. Only a stone-hearted man could not react with delight to see the deity of Lord Jagannatha drawn on his huge cart, surrounded by hundreds of chanting devotees."

In Berkeley, California, a Lord Caitanya Festival was held to celebrate Caitanya's appearance day. The festivities were dominated by a twenty-foot form of the Lord, who was carried on a platform atop the shoulders of his devotees. After a procession and a kirtana, the devotees introduced transcendental theatre with two plays, "Big Fish, Little Fish" and "The Saga of Liquid Beauty." A devotee commented, "These plays were filled with the Lord's presence and thus they were filled with humor, knowledge, and transcendental pleasure."

In Boston a butter churning festival was held, not for any special occasion, but for the purpose of attracting attention to the temple, the devotees, and their activities. As with every festival, publicity of all kinds was sought—posters, newspaper coverage, radio and television coverage. "Public festivals held for the glorification of the Lord are a unique happy process by which many, many people can achieve bhakti-yoga. If the festival is pleasing and people respond to nice chanting, decorated carts, and prasada, then they are actually appreciating Krsna himself; and by such appreciation, all can attain pure devotional service. That's the transcendental meaning of the festivals," said a brahmacari. On a more practical note, the president of the Boston temple said, "We will try anything to trick people into participation in Krsna Consciousness."

Following every special event, there is always discussion among the devotees about how "blissful" the ceremonies were, and exaggerated claims about how many people joined in and how ecstatic the proceedings were. A description of a Lord Caitanya Festival from *Back to Godhead* (No. 35, p. 16) magazine is typical:

> Overcome by the sight of the Lord, the devotees fell to their knees and offered repeated obeisances. Some members of the gathered crowd, which now numbered several thousand, also fell to their knees, and others became silent

and shy in the presence of the Lord. After proper respects had been offered, kirtana began, more ecstatic than before, and thousands of spirit souls danced blissfully around the Lord. How could any man hope to describe the happiness that was felt?

If one attends any of these festivities, he will observe the devotees dancing ecstatically, while most of the crowd silently observes the occasion. A few spectators usually join in. When a visitor to the temple has participated with a particularly flamboyant display, the devotees are later heard to remark that the visitor appeared crazy. Indeed, some of the devotees have been observed snickering during wild performances. Some devotees may laugh if they feel that a visitor's actions are a mockery of their own behavior.

5 / Transcendental mechanics: practical aspects of temple life

> I offer my humble obeisances unto His Divine Grace Prabhupada A. C. Bhakti-vedanta Swami . . .
> who danced to Krsna beneath the sun in L.A. and beneath the red, white and blue flashing neon illusions of Hollywood Blvd., Kali-Yuga plastic America, and beneath the moon danced to Govinda and Radharani in a Manhattan alley, searching for a possible temple,
> who proclaimed natural vegetarian prasadamism to the nation's hamburger stands, the cow-eaters of America, the pig-eaters, the bird-eaters, fish-eaters, lamb-eaters, threatening them with endless rebirths as tigers,
> who must laugh at the maya karmaval, the vast play of illusion, of America, of the world. (Hayagriva dasa Adhikari)

The communal life within an ISKCON temple falls into Goffman's (1961: xiii) criteria for total institutions (see Chapter 1). Belief in the ideology is the binding factor for the devotees, who voluntarily submit themselves to temple life and discipline for the purpose of furthering their common goal—the performance of bhakti.

In this sense all members of ISKCON are equal. But practically the organization has a hierarchical political structure to administer the bureaucratic organization of what Goffman (1961: 6) calls "whole blocks of people." The supervisory people, however, are also full-time devotees who live in the temple and have restricted contact with the outside world. In this way the ISKCON administration differs from Goffman's (1961: 7) supervisory staff, who typically operate on an eight-hour day, are socially integrated into the outside world, and maintain a greater social distance from the larger managed group. There is a certain restriction on the passage of information from the supervisory devotees to the devotees as a group. For the most part, however, because of the integrative effect of the ideology, the split between supervisory devotees and the rest of the devotees is insignificant on the structural level. To achieve an understanding of the interpersonal interactions within the temple, we will begin with an examination of the political structure.

POLITICAL STRUCTURE

The formal political structure of the sixty-three (or more) temples[1] and approximately three thousand members[2] of ISKCON is based on social control through the

---

[1] See Appendix IV for a list of ISKCON temples.

[2] The number, three thousand, is the movement's official estimate. No records are kept, and people go in and out of the movement at a rapid rate. See footnote 3 in the Introduction.

use of authority. All authority technically rests with the spiritual master. He, as God's representative on earth, is the last resort and the ultimate authority in all conflict solutions and questions of doctrine and practice. As the devotees have stated, "The order of Prabhupada is to be taken as one's life and soul." In August 1970, Bhaktivedanta Swami decided to establish a governing body commission, called the GBC, creating a formal structure for ISKCON. The precipitating reasons for the establishment of the GBC were Bhaktivedanta Swami's advanced age, his poor health,[3] and the rapid growth of the movement. The GBC was established in a letter sent to temple presidents which was not circulated among the devotees, although they were informed of the letter and the establishment of the GBC. The past president of the Boston temple described the letter to the researcher as a "document dividing the world into twelve zones, six of which are in the U.S. and Canada and six in Europe and Asia." Twelve men devotees, who were considered by Prabhupada to have outstanding managerial talents and to be very advanced in Krsna Consciousness, were appointed to relieve him of managerial tasks. Their main tasks are to decide where new centers will be established[4] and who will be sent to open them, to insure that the temples are following Bhaktivedanta Swami's orders and ceremonies, and to maintain high standards in all temples.

The letter creating the GBC opened with a description of how Prabhupada came to the United States, opened one temple, and how the movement grew gradually and spread. Prabhupada explained that he is now seventy-four years old and may leave the scene at any moment so he will create this managing body, known as the GBC, and he hopes that the devotees will kindly accept this. These men will be his personal representatives. As long as he is here they will be his zonal secretaries; after he leaves they will be known as his executors. In the future, the temple presidents will elect the GBC members for terms of three years each. GBC members can serve more than one term if reelected. All temple presidents will meet at least once a year on Janmastami and at various other times whenever necessary.

This researcher can only guess why the president did not want to show this letter, but it is probable that the letter specified what should happen in the event of Bhaktivedanta Swami's death. When asked about this, the president made it plain that "a spiritual master will simply emerge—just as Prabhupada emerged." Since the spiritual master is not a material body and his appearance is on the authority of God, the devotees are not allowed to speculate on future events. But on another occasion the president said to the researcher that he does not have to worry about Prabhupada's disappearance "because we have our instructions and we have the GBC. The devotees can rest assured that the GBC will give direction."

The line of authority extends from the regional GBC member to the president of the temple, who is responsible for seeing that the orders of the spiritual master and the GBC are carried out in his temple. He is also responsible for his devotees much as a father is responsible for his children. Like the head of a household, he must be able to settle disputes, offer spiritual guidance, delegate authority, assign work, and advise devotees on practical, everyday problems that arise. It is he who decides who may stay in the temple and who may not, and this authority may be

[3] Bhaktivedanta Swami has suffered at least one stroke.
[4] Bhaktivedanta Swami has asked for one hundred and eight temples before he leaves this planet, one for each of the one hundred and eight japa beads upon which the devotees chant.

exercised without recourse. For instance, a fifteen-year-old female devotee appeared one day from the Atlanta, Georgia, temple, where she had been expelled due to a personality conflict with the temple pujari. After a week in the Boston temple, she was asked by the president to leave; no reason was given, and the girl claimed that she had no idea what the reason might be.

The president has the power to call an ista-gosti whenever he deems it necessary. These meetings are a kind of gripe session in which temple problems can be discussed. A typical ista-gosti agenda might include a talk by the pujari admonishing the devotees for their behavior at aratrika, complaints about using the mops from the deity closet on floors other than the temple room, thus rendering them impure for temple room and altar use, bathroom rules, new rules that must be put into effect, schedule changes, allocation of tasks, and things as mundane as spending laksmi (money) for Hydrox cookies and Mars bars.

The temple president states that caring for the deities is his main function, and in addition he is given complete authority in all temple business. The president must be informed of all business matters and spending decisions. He plays the role of father confessor, is responsible for the health of the devotees, is the congregation leader, and the authority on scripture and ceremonies. Even the personal decisions of the devotees come under his jurisdiction. During a typical day the president may be called upon to decide what truck to buy for temple transportation, and spend the morning calling automobile dealers to check prices. A woman devotee might come to him to ask his permission to leave the temple to visit her mother; and if he says no, as he often does, she will change her plans. It is typical for a devotee to call the president, as has been done, from a laundromat because there was more laundry than anticipated and the devotees delegated to the laundry tasks were not given enough money. On that occasion, the president was heard to say impatiently, "Well you have some girls with you, don't you? Go out and beg!" He will spend an hour or two on the phone trying to drum up donations, or calling schools, other religious groups, and newspapers, inviting people to the temple for a feast. He can tell a devotee who has not been well to see the doctor on the itinerant medical van. Most temple presidents observed by this researcher were outstanding in their managerial talents, but one or two of them have had trouble managing the interpersonal relationships over and above the usual personal conflicts. Some of the devotees have mentioned that a temple is run like a military regime, commenting on the rigid schedule observance and the necessity of being able to take orders.

The president of the Boston temple has summed up his role as follows:

> It is my business to engage people in service by discovering their best qualifications and what they like to do and suit this to time and circumstance. It is also my duty to collect money for the temple—this is part of managing. I also am father, advisor, confessor. I am father to the children because I represent the real father, Prabhupada.

There is no strict formalized method of recruiting temple presidents. A retiring president will often choose his successor before quitting office, or the decision may be left to Prabhupada or the GBC if the retiring president does not make a choice. Any advanced devotee may volunteer to start a temple if he can raise the money. If a temple president needs additional managerial assistance, he may appoint a temple commander, who may sometimes also assume the duties of sankirtana leader. In addition, various tasks are allocated to specific people such as the pujari, who directs the work of the women assigned to sewing, garland making, and deity work, and the cook, who is in charge of the kitchen.

Not subject to the jurisdiction of any particular temple are the sannyasis, a very spiritually advanced order who have special austerities and special responsibilities. These sannyasis are completely independent of everyone in the movement except the spiritual master. The special duties of the sannyasis are to study scripture and preach; therefore they are not attached to a temple but travel around, especially to new territories. When one of ISKCON's sannyasis visits a temple, he is expected to enliven the devotees in the temple. The temple presidents work with the sannyasis as well as with the GBC and accord all respect to sannyasis as a higher authority. A sannyasi who has renounced the material world travels about accepting as students those who are seriously inclined toward Krsna Consciousness. All devotees give special service to a sannyasi, offering their obeisances each morning when he appears and giving him a special room in which to stay while visiting the temple. If a sannyasi will allow it, one or more devotees will attach themselves to him as his personal servants.

CONFLICT AND FACTIONALISM

The primary method of social control rests with authority vested in the temple presidents, the sannyasis, and the GBC as a body. However, the spiritual master or any of them may resort to the most serious sanction—expulsion—if it is believed to be warranted in a particular situation. It is expulsion that is invoked in every case of severe conflict or serious breach of faith.

The most serious conflict observed by the researcher took place on Janmastami in New Vrndavana in August 1970. The conflict occurred during the presidents' meeting at a time when many devotees had come a long way for the Janmastami festival. After mangala-aratrika, four sannyasis announced that Srila Prabhupada was fed up with his American boys and girls and that they must try harder to learn to follow his teachings. As an example they used the Boston temple, which they claimed was heavily in maya. The president of the Boston temple, Ramanuji, was furious, and the conflict that ensued almost caused the movement to fall apart. A whole group departed to confer in the woods, and when they returned one sannyasi said, "Prabhupada had conned all of the devotees" and that "he was only a common man." The four sannyasis wanted to take over the movement; but after a discussion about who Prabhupada was, Ramanuja and the other temple presidents were able to gain control and sway most of the devotees back to the movement's original position on the guru. The four sannyasis were expelled, but it was later made clear that if they were willing to admit they had made a mistake, they would be welcomed back into the movement. Many devotees quit the movement in the days following this discussion. After the event a series of ista-gostis were held at the Boston temple based on the question of who was Srila Prabhupada. It was finally decided that the guru is not God but is God's representative. The devotees should not speculate, they should just accept him. He is not an ordinary person and through him Krsna is working. For those who did not quit, life went on as usual, and the event was forgotten completely.

Disagreements are simply not tolerated in a temple. Even if they are personal in nature, they should be subdued in an effort to better serve Krsna. If a person's behavior is offensive to the other devotees or if he is not cooperating, then social pressure will be brought to bear from the group. The offender will be lectured by one or more devotees in an effort to urge him to conform. He will be chastized gently at first, but if the behavior continues, the devotees will grow continually more insistent. In some cases where there is personal disagreement and conflict, an individual will move to another temple. For example, a devotee who could not get along with her husband left the Boston temple and went to the New York temple with her child. Another husband and wife who had conflicts with the temple president and some individual devotees in the Boston temple left and also went to the New York temple. There is a pujari in the movement so difficult to please that "she has gone through many women devotees," who claim "she hassled them" and they moved on.

Conflict is always subdued by the devotees, and they generally try to keep outsiders from learning that all is not sweetness and light. In general, the devotees present a united front to the public, and problems are never openly discussed if outsiders are visiting.

ECONOMIC ACTIVITIES

An ISKCON brahmacari begging on the streets is a common sight in cities where temples exist. A sankirtana party goes out daily from the temple to chant in the streets, and every devotee is expected to participate regularly in sankirtana to bring "Lord Caitanya's message to every town and village." The devotees go out carrying mrdangas, karatals, prasada, and stacks of *Back to Godhead*. Some devotees chant and dance while others fan out to sell *Back to Godhead* magazines. The idea is "to interest passers-by in the magazine without getting involved in long nit-picking theological discussions." A contribution of fifty cents or a dollar is requested for the magazine, but a quarter would be accepted on the advice of the spiritual master, who said, "Every gentleman has a quarter." If there is no possibility of selling the magazine, the brahmacaris try to beg for a contribution anyway. In addition to begging on the street, phone calls are made to local citizens and to any friends of ISKCON by the president in an effort to urge them to contribute. Most of the devotees who keep in touch with their families regularly ask them for donations. At the Sunday feasts everyone is asked to contribute a dollar, but if a person cannot do this, he is never pressured to do so. The magazine is often given free to people who say they have no money but who appear genuinely interested in it. Each copy of *Back to Godhead* is purchased by the temple for nineteen cents. The magazine contains no advertising and is written and edited in New York, sent to Los Angeles to be printed, and returned to New York to be put together. The individual temple can keep a small amount of the money earned from *Back to Godhead*, but the rest goes to Prabhupada's book fund. Each temple also sells his books whenever possible, and all book profits from temple sales are sent to the book fund.

Many members sell Bhaktivedanta Swami's books on the street to earn their living. For example, when a *Srimad-Bhagavatam* costing five dollars is sold for ten dollars the seller can keep the five-dollar profit for his own living expenses if he is a householder or if he wants to earn his fare to India. (Many devotees want to go to India to work on Bhaktivedanta Swami's projects there.) If the devotee lives in a temple he will turn the profits from his book sales over to his temple.

Each temple is allowed to use the money earned from incense sales to pay its expenses. However, all money over and above these expenses should be sent to the Bhaktivedanta Book Trust, along with all profits the temple has made from selling books and magazines, and from other business ventures. The money sent to the Book Trust is spent for the publication of Bhaktivedanta Swami's books, for the construction or purchase of temples, and for food relief programs in distressed areas of India. A financial statement[5] was issued by the Boston temple, but it is only accurate enough to give the sketchiest details of expenses, since items such as telephone expenditures, cost of fresh flowers, and laundry costs are not included. Since this date the incense sales have increased dramatically, and the temple can meet its deep monthly debts. It is the policy of all temples to extend themselves financially as far as possible. An Indian businessman has contributed to the London temple and has inquired into the devotees' financial transactions in order to advise them. He believes that although the devotees are sincere and doing well in worship of God, they have no idea how to manage their financial affairs prudently. He accuses them of failing to plan ahead and of overextending their credit. He thinks that the devotees' grandiose plans to move to a bigger and better temple are impractical and definitely beyond their means. When the businessman tried to urge the devotees to give up such expensive plans they told him, "Krsna provides." "Sure," he said, "Krsna provides, but it helps to be practical. The devotees refuse to listen to reason and are going on with their scheme for the new temple. I am getting a bit disgusted with their constant financial crises."

The persistent financial crises are faced by the devotees with an easy calm, "Krsna provides" and "Krsna Consciousness is always a crisis." A devotee in the Boston temple reported, "When Srila Prabhupada came to our temple he looked up at the broken windows and said, 'Is this our temple?' " Later some devotees were heard remarking to the president, "When will we be moving to a better temple? Is this a proper home for Krsna?"

ISKCON press is run on a small profit margin, most of which is reinvested in printing more of Prabhupada's books. All press devotees work at least an eight-hour day, seven days a week, at unsalaried jobs keeping the cost of the books very low for the quality offered. For instance, the profusely and colorfully illustrated *Krsna* book (Bhaktivedanta Swami 1971) sells for eight dollars while a book of comparable quality published by a karmi publisher would cost at least fifteen dollars. The press operation is a thoroughly professional organization with an expert printing staff, presses, a full painting staff for illustrations, photographers, and developing equipment. The press is housed in a renovated warehouse a few blocks from the temple in New York. The head pressman, who had previously spent a two-year apprenticeship in a professional printing plant on the spiritual master's orders, runs a tight shop. He writes up each task scheduled for the day on cards labeled "Transcendental Job Ticket." Two offset presses work long hours printing Bhaktivedanta Swami's books. It is here that Srila Prabhupada's often faulty English is polished.

[5] See Appendix V for a financial statement of March 1972 issued by the Boston temple.

Devotees are discouraged from seeking outside jobs, although in emergency situations some men have taken jobs as teachers, social workers, and factory workers long enough to raise money for a specific goal. It was through the combined employment of three devotees that the original ISKCON printing press was purchased. There are some pressmen who live outside the temple with their wives and children and these householders are encouraged to start businesses. Some of these wives have gotten together to produce some confections made of nuts and dried fruits, which they are selling successfully to health food stores and specialty shops around New York City to meet rent expenses. Another pressman has started a private printing business, but he still spends a few evenings a week working on Prabhupada's books, and his wife and child still spend most of their waking hours at the temple. Sometimes men who were starting new temples have had to be employed to raise the funds for rent, food, and initial expenses; but they have left their jobs when they have enough full-time devotees to make a go of the temple without outside employment. Some devotees sell Indian clothing and gift items. Still others sell flowers on the street.

Bhaktivedanta Swami's stated intention is that each person should remain in his occupation or station in life, but that he should use whatever capacity or talent he or she has and dovetail it with Krsna Consciousness. So the writer may write articles for Krsna. Householders raise children in Krsna Consciousness, and husband and wife should live in mutual cooperation for spiritual progress. Businessmen are encouraged to become life-time members at $1111.00 and may, in this way, participate in ISKCON without abandoning their occupation. There are a few life members, but in most cases their participation is not regular. Other people have become members by donating $4.50 for a one-year membership, $555.00 for a donor mem-

A devotee offering prasada to the public and requesting a donation.

ber, and $222.00 for a subscriber member who gets a lifetime subscription to *Back to Godhead* magazine.

Although the devotees say that they would prefer to sit under a tree and chant all day, the movement's missionary work nevertheless demands a cash flow. The real backbone of ISKCON's economic success is the Spiritual Sky Incense Company, which manufactures and distributes incense. In one short year the company's profits have risen from one million dollars in 1973 to at least double that in 1974.

All incense manufacturing is done in Los Angeles by a crew of ten devotees in a small cinder block factory. Producing the incense is a very simple process in which the incense sticks and cones are dipped in fragrant oils and readied for shipping. With only thirty-five full-time employees (and a computer that continuously prints out the Hare Krsna mantra when not otherwise employed), the company must farm out most labelling, packaging, and production of other products. Spiritual Sky sells other scented products (made for them by Avon), including oils, shampoo, and soap. None of these toiletries are cheap. A two and one-half ounce bar of soap costs one dollar retail and a package of twelve incense sticks goes for $1.25.

The bulk of the business is wholesaling incense to retail shops outside of Krsna Consciousness. Warehouses are maintained in Los Angeles, New York, New Orleans, and Dallas. Spiritual Sky wholesales its products to the individual temples at a markup of 11 percent over cost. The temples then sell to stores at double their cost, and the retail cost is double that. Each temple is financially independent, and the one or two devotees who sell the incense provide most of the support for a temple's activities.

Some incense is sold by professional salesmen and some by devotee salesmen. To most retailers the yellow-robed salesmen present an amusing image. The devotees report that they find no problem with "head shops" and boutiques, but in "straight places like department stores, the buyers sometimes freak out and worry about what their customers are going to think." Consequently, for such encounters the devotees wear wigs and ordinary business suits. Some allow their hair to grow into a crew cut.

Professional salesmen are hired whenever ISKCON's national marketing manager decides that they are needed to get optimum sales from a territory. These men receive commissions that are competitive with other sales positions in non-Hare Krsna firms. Each salesman receives a salary, a car, insurance, an expense account, and commissions. Recently more karmi salesmen have been hired to give the devotees more time to practice devotional activities.

The incense business is incorporated separately as Spiritual Sky Scented Products. As in all other matters, Bhaktivedanta Swami is the ultimate authority in Spiritual Sky. The incense company is managed by a president, some vice presidents, a national sales manager, and regional sales managers. Except for advertising consultants and some hired salesmen, all of the employees of Spiritual Sky are devotees. Devotees manage the business at the higher levels, and the practical work is handled both by devotees and hired people.

Bhaktivedanta Swami (1968: *Bhagavad-gita* 12:10) explains his views on public involvement and ISKCON's economic activities as follows:

> One should be sympathetic to the propagation of Krsna Consciousness. There are many devotees who are engaged in the propagation of Krsna Consciousness

and they require help. So even if one cannot directly practice the regulated principles of bhakti-yoga, he can try to help such propaganda work. Every endeavor requires land, capital, organization and labor. Just as in business, one requires a place to stay, some capital to use, some labor and some organization to make propaganda, so the same is required in the service of Krsna. The only difference is that materialism means to work for sense gratification. The same work, however, can be performed for the satisfaction of Krsna: that is spiritual activity.

The belief that work becomes spiritual activity provides a strong motivation for high performance and dedication on the part of a devotee. The essential needs of temple devotees are provided for, so their motives and attitudes toward work differ from karmi workers who, upon receipt of a paycheck, go their own way. The devotees who are lucky enough to have their talents, interests, and capabilities dovetail with Krsna-conscious activity can become quickly and deeply integrated into the movement, and that can aid in their spiritual development.

SOCIALIZATION OF DEVOTEES

The ISKCON temple provides an institutional setting which allows its members a well-defined ideological and structural situation as well as formal rites and positive identifications and models. The spiritual master calls himself an acarya, which means teacher by example, and following in the footsteps of the great acaryas is the goal of all devotees. Bhaktivedanta Swami (1970b: 60) directs:

> . . . that a devotee follow the past acaryas and saintly persons because by such following one can achieve the desired results, with no chance of lamenting or being baffled in his progress.

All devotees wish to become great acaryas, and entrance into a temple and following the regulative principles of bhakti are the recommended methods of achieving this goal. The temple is an educational arena where an individual is socialized into the terminology and strategies necessary for living in the temple setting apart from the rest of society.

A new devotee entering a temple is assigned to one or more devotees who show him how to behave and explain temple rules and regulations to him. There are four rules of conduct which must be observed by all devotees. These rules which are the cornerstone of a regulated life are:

1. No gambling. This rule also excludes frivolous sports and games. In addition, devotees are advised not to engage in any conversation that is not connected with the teachings of Krsna Consciousness or with the execution of duties. All other speech or reading is called mental speculation and is a luxury in which the devotees do not engage.
2. No intoxicants. This rule includes all narcotics, alcoholic beverages, tobacco, coffee, and tea. ISKCON's efficiency in getting its members to abandon the use of drugs such as marijuana, LSD, and others, has drawn commendations from the mayors of New York and San Francisco. Medicines may be taken when absolutely necessary, but whenever possible medicines containing narcotic substances should be avoided. In actual practice, the devotees discourage the use of any and all medicines. If absolutely unavoidable, devotees will see a doctor and take medicine, but chanting the Hare Krsna mantra is con-

sidered to be a better remedy for bodily ills. The devotees feel that bodily ills are Krsna's mercy because the illness reminds them "that they are not this body."

3. No illicit sex. Sexual relations are permitted only between individuals married by a qualified devotee in Krsna Consciousness. There is no dating or courtship allowed. Marriage is an arrangement for two devotees of Krsna to serve and worship in this way. A swami stated it succinctly: "If a devotee believes he can serve Krsna better by being married, then he gets married. Marriage is primarily for the purpose of raising children in Krsna Consciousness."

4. No eating of meat, fish, or eggs. The only food that can be eaten by devotees is food prepared under strict dietary regulations and offered by prescribed ceremony to Krsna. When traveling or under unusual circumstances, devotees may eat foods such as fruit or milk which can easily be offered and which do not necessarily require preparation; under no circumstances may unoffered food be eaten. In ISKCON, eating is an act of worship and must be conducted accordingly.

Breaking any of these rules could result in expulsion from ISKCON as could the blatant refusal to follow the orders of the spiritual master or a temple president. Speaking against the spiritual master, blaspheming God, contradicting scripture are additional offenses punishable by expulsion.

The practice of bhakti begins with these regulative principles which one follows by order of the spiritual master or the strength of regulative principles. There can be no question of refusal. The second or developed stage of bhakti comes when the bhakta, by following the regulative principles, becomes more attached to Krsna and executes devotional service out of natural love and real attachment. Spontaneous love and service should grow out of following regulative principles and chanting the Hare Krsna mantra. Chanting is said to have so much power that it immediately attaches one to Krsna, through its transcendental sound vibrations.

A new devotee is taught to follow temple rules and regulations: how to behave in the temple during ceremonies, how to prostrate himself before the deities, how to say various prayers and hymns in Sanskrit, how to eat with his fingers Indian-style, how to maintain temple standards of cleanliness and hygiene, how to do a job if he does not already have a skill, how to chant, how to follow temple routine, and how to use a vocabulary of Sanskrit words that will replace karmi words. Entrance into a temple also means a shift to communal living. Although some married couples live outside the temple, most devotees live within temple walls. The devotees eat together, chant and dance together, work together, and sleep together. There is no furniture in a temple other than the spiritual master's vyasasana, a few desks, and a small table or two to hold religious articles. There are no chairs except those used for elderly guests, so all desks and tables used for work are sawed down to floor-sitting size. At night the devotees unroll sleeping bags and sleep on the floor, men in one section of the temple and women in another. Most activities are what Goffman calls "batch activities." Due to the nature of their communal life, the devotees say they have no private life and that Krsna Consciousness is an open secret. Austerity and group living are the two main features of temple life to which a new devotee must quickly accustom himself. In some temples the austerity practiced due to lack of economic resources is formidable. For example, in Boston the devotees lived without heat for six months in the winter of 1971–1972.

The clean-up.

In Amsterdam, there is no running water for showers, and devotees shower by pouring cold water over themselves with buckets. At New Vrndavana, West Virginia, the devotees live without heat, running water, or any of the amenities. They are slowly adding sanitation facilities, but the austerity will remain. At times of great austerity, the devotees will eat less—just some cooked cereal for breakfast, dahl and capatis for lunch, and milk and cookies at night. One day after eating dahl and capatis every day for weeks at noon, one sincere devotee told me that Prabhupada said dahl and capatis are a perfect diet for those going outdoors for sankirtana every day. This cheerful attitude toward austerity is typical.

A male devotee entering a temple must be prepared to shave his head except for a remaining lock of hair called the sikha. It is said that for thousands of years devotees of Krsna have worn their hair in this way as a sign of surrender to the spiritual master who is pleased to see his disciples entering into Krsna-conscious life. The devotees say that the purpose of the sikha is to enable Krsna to pull them out of maya, should they happen to fall into her clutches. It is also a haircut which avoids any preening that might foster a false ego. To the public such visible signs as the sikha are constant reminders that the devotees of God are present, and therefore the sikha puts God directly in the mind of all who see it. The sikha is one of the few modes of personal expression for male devotees. Some are worn longer and braided, others knotted, others flowing, some sikhas are thick and others are thin. A sikha is not worn by the few devotees who hold jobs on the outside.

Men wear a dhoti, a long draped garment worn in place of pants. This is topped by a long, loose Indian shirt slit at both sides with a long one-sided cape tied at the right shoulder, falling like a drape to the knees. There are variations on this theme. Sometimes the cape is not worn at all or a tee shirt or sweater will be used. In winter long underwear and heavy socks are worn. Since the devotees do not wear leather, their shoes are either canvas or plastic. In winter they present an odd picture with the long thermal underwear hanging below the dhotis, wearing tennis shoes, and heavy ski jackets. For some types of heavy work, such as press work, pants are worn because a dhoti could be dangerous.

Women devotees all wear the traditional Indian garment, a sari over a shirt-like slip. Under the sari a blouse, sweater, or tee shirt is worn, which is properly modest and high-necked. The sari is rarely draped over the shoulder, but worn covering the head and pinned at the side of the cheek. In hot weather or at work, the sari may be draped over the shoulder rather than covering the head. If a sari is inconvenient for some types of work, a long dress or skirt will be worn instead. Pants are never worn. Jewelry is very popular, especially pierced earrings, bracelets, necklaces, and pins. At times ankle bracelets are worn and noses may be pierced to wear a stud-type jewel or a nose ring through the middle of the nostrils. All women wear their hair parted in the center and braided. If they are married, they smear a red makeup into the part of their hair.

All devotees go barefoot in the temple unless it is so cold that they are forced to wear socks, but this is not desirable. No leather goods are worn or used. Each devotee always carries a string of one hundred eight japa beads which are usually carried in a bead bag worn around the neck, convenient for chanting the mahamantra in spare moments. Devotees also wear small beads made of tulasi, the sacred plant, around their necks. These are called kunti-mala and signify a lifetime commitment to Vaisnavism. Tilaka (clay markings) are also worn on the body to mark it as a temple. The most prominent mark is worn on the forehead and bears a resemblance to an exclamation mark, going from the hairline and ending in a point on the nose. Some devotees will write Hare Krsna with wet tilaka on the body, and all mark twelve places on the body with tilaka for sanctification and protection. The body is marked at the forehead, abdomen, chest, throat, right waist, right forearm, right shoulder, left waist, left forearm, left shoulder, nape of the neck, and lower back. All married devotees wear bright yellow dhotis or saris, and all unmarried celibate devotees wear a saffron-colored dhoti or sari.

It was mentioned earlier that the devotee must learn to follow the orders of the spiritual master and in his absence the orders of his representatives, the temple presidents, and those he delegates as task leaders. One ex-devotee (blooper) notes that

> . . . they never tell you what you are in for. The devotees just tell you that everything is lovely and blissful. Everything is super high, everything is bliss! They never tell you that everyone will be throwing orders at you from all sides. Somehow the idea of always having to take orders gave me troubles. I'd do a thing for a while—if it was something bad—that went against the grain, I simply wouldn't do it. I'd try to explain why—to give reasons why I didn't want to do

the thing. Sometimes they would listen. Sometimes they would try to convince me to do the thing. "Oh Prabhu, you want to be saved. You don't want to fall into maya." They would always use a soft tone of voice. Sometimes they could be so sweet and convincing that you would do the thing so you'd be like them.

At first, they'd give you flower garlands in the morning to wear and everyone talked to you and told you nice stories about Krsna. If you had troubles they tried to talk to you and make you feel wanted for a while. Then later, everyone gets into their thing. They begin to reprimand you, but very nicely, each evening.

Other devotees accept all orders willingly: "I know that I am not doing this for the pujari; I am doing this for Krsna. Why should I let her bug me? I have to learn to serve Krsna better."

Potential devotees are usually encouraged to visit the temple regularly for about a month so that they can adjust gradually to temple life, but this practice may be bypassed. Some devotees have come to the Sunday feast and decided to stay. One boy came every day for a month at 4:00 A.M. after sleeping in the park each night, before he was allowed to move into the temple. A girl was brought by her friends to the temple while having a bad trip on LSD; the devotees accepted her and she stayed. When a person wants to come into a temple, there are no hard and fast procedures to be followed. The president can accept or reject a potential devotee. Most people who are interested have already read the *Gita* or tried chanting. If the would-be devotee is not serious, he will usually leave within a couple of days. The only demand at first is that the four temple rules are strictly observed. Since everyone is coming from maya's camp the devotees are lenient. New devotees are considered to be like wild animals and are given kind and gentle treatment. It is a mark of a good devotee to be kind and gentle at all times. After a devotee has been in a temple for a while and has proved himself to be a sincere devotee, the temple president may write to Prabhupada recommending that this devotee be initiated. If Prabhupada cannot be present at the initiation, he will chant his rounds on the devotee's beads and give him his spiritual name. The beads and a letter are sent to the temple president who will preside over a fire ceremony for the formal harernama, or holy name initiation. Each letter begins by saying the devotee is "duly initiated" and goes on to tell his new name and its auspicious meanings. Until recently, a devotee did not have to wait the prescribed six months to be initiated. If the temple president thought the devotee was ready, he could write to Prabhupada requesting the initiation. Lately, however, Bhaktivedanta Swami has suggested that the potential initiates wait at least six months because so many initiated devotees were blooping (dropping out of the movement). In each temple it is necessary to have a certain number of initiated devotees to perform certain tasks such as cooking since only an initiated devotee can touch the stove except in extreme emergencies.

Six months after the devotee passes his harer-nama ceremony, he becomes eligible for his second initiation, which is celebrated with a fire ceremony.[6] Through this ceremony the devotee becomes a brahmin by receiving the sacred thread and a secret mantra, the gayatri mantra, which is never to be uttered aloud because it may be an inauspicious moment. During the fire ceremony each initiate

_____

[6] This ceremony is the same as the fire ceremony used to celebrate a marriage. See the section in this chapter on marriage for a description of the rite.

receives his sacred thread, which is worn over the left shoulder passing diagonally across the chest. The person conducting the ceremony places the thread on the bare chest of the men. Women do not receive a sacred thread. Next each initiate is passed a tape recorder and earphones so he can listen to the gayatri mantra. The initiate now is able to perform certain ceremonies such as aratrika and fire ceremonies when necessary, and is considered to be a priest of ISKCON. Here again, although a six-month period should elapse before the second initiation, the waiting period may be bypassed if deemed necessary by Bhaktivedanta Swami or the temple president.

Bhaktivedanta Swami (1970b: 4) states:

> A person is born in a brahmana family or in a family of dog-eaters, due to his past activities. If a person is born in a family of dog-eaters, it means that his past activities are all sinful. But if even such a person takes to the path of devotional service and begins to chant the holy name of the Lord, he is at once fit to perform the ritualistic ceremonies. This means his sinful reactions have immediately become neutralized.

The regulative principles are applicable to people in every stage of spiritual life. According to the Vedic system, a man's life is divided into four parts:

1. Brahmacari—celibate student
2. Grhastha—householder, married man
3. Vanaprastha—retired order
4. Sannyasi, swami—renounced order of life

The first part is the student's life which is meant for creating a spirit of detachment through knowledge, renunciation, and devotion to the Lord. During this period, the student remains celibate, studies under the spiritual master, and serves him. For those who fail to develop sufficient detachment during the first stage, the second stage is married life. Many new devotees enter the temple already married and immediately become householders. Sex is allowed under certain restrictions, and a sense of detachment should be present. The third stage is the retired life. During this period the householder leaves home to prepare himself for complete detachment. The wife can accompany him as a voluntary servant, but they have no sex life. The renounced order of life is the final stage. When the man becomes fully detached from sex life, he sends his wife home to be taken care of by the oldest son, and he becomes a mendicant. This is illustrated in the life of Bhaktivedanta Swami. Some students who never enter the married stage of life go directly to this stage if Prabhupada feels that they are suited for sannyasa life. They may receive the title of Swami meaning "one who controls his senses." There is a fire ceremony conducted by Bhaktivedanta Swami when a man takes sannyasa.

New devotees are expected to learn by the example of the great acaryas; they are taught how to dress, eat, and live according to Vedic prescription. They are indoctrinated into an ideology which recognizes the necessity of eating, sleeping, mating, and defending, but teaches that these activities should be restricted and simplified to leave time and energy for spiritual pursuits, which should be the only focus of a devotee's life. In order to learn this philosophy all members must attend classes. When necessary, there are special classes held for new devotees. All devotees are also urged to read as much authorized scripture as possible when they have time.

The classes are designed to help the devotees better understand the scriptures and answer their questions. In the words of a woman devotee: "In New York we had our *Gita* class with the curtains open. It was wonderful for me because I realized that was the same Krsna present as we had been reading about. My questions were answered, and I knew why I was doing devotional service."

New devotees are taught a rich new Sanskrit vocabulary from the other devotees through their reading and from listening to the tapes of the guru. The speech habits of Prabhupada are transmitted in these ways, so it is common to hear such expressions as, "Oh, bliss," "I will take rest," "Now we will take prasada," "Please give me laksmi for streetcar fare," and one of the guru's favorite adjectives, "nice," is used *ad nauseum* by the devotees. The devotees also enjoy imitating his inflections and tendency to quote scripture in Sanskrit. Once a devotee was quoting a Sanskrit phrase to a visitor who asked,

"Do you know what that means?"
"No, but I read it in scripture."

Sanskrit is the language spoken in Krsna–loka and the spiritual sky. It is regarded as a holy language, having special auspicious properties which aid in the advancement of a devotee's spiritual progress. The terminologies are an important means of reinforcing the culture pattern of Krsna Consciousness and socializing a new devotee into it.

MARRIAGE

The position of ISKCON regarding marriage has undergone great changes since the organization's beginning years. At first marriage was regarded (as it is in India) as the foundation institution of society, and marriage between devotees was encouraged. If either Bhaktivedanta Swami or a temple president felt that a devotee should marry, he would ask that devotee to marry a specific person. Some presidents told me that they could order a devotee to marry if they saw fit. A devotee could ask the permission of his temple president if he wanted to get married. Some devotees would ask to marry a specific person, and the president could refuse or grant the request as he wished. Other devotees, who had split with their karmi spouses, were encouraged to dissolve any legal ties and remarry an ISKCON member. A couple will usually be married in a civil ceremony before joining the temple if they want to join together, so many couples who had been living together before entering the temple were married. Couples who were about to marry in ISKCON would be married in a civil ceremony before they had their ISKCON ceremony in the temple to avoid any tangles with the law.

A Krsna-conscious marriage is sanctified with an impressive and beautiful fire sacrificial ceremony. The couple prepare by buying new clothes, and the bride has her face painted according to Vedic custom. The devotees and the guests gather in the temple to witness the ceremony. The priest and the couple wear garlands of flowers which have been touched to the feet of the deities. The audience begins to chant the Hare Krsna mantra and continues chanting throughout the ceremony when no other prayers are being said. After the responsive chanting begins the rite with a lecture on the importance of marriage. Following the lecture the woman's parent or a godbrother gives her into the care of the bridegroom, who promises "to take charge" of her throughout both of their lives and that there will never be any separation or divorce. The bride then promises to serve the man always and to help him carry out his Krsna-conscious activities. The couple exchange garlands and sitting places. The groom places vermillion in the part of his bride's hair and covers her head with her sari. The priest ties the husband's dhoti to the bride's sari, a knot which is supposed to remain tied for one week.

Next the priest sprinkles different colored dyes over the dirt upon which the fire is to be made. With a candle he lights a stick dipped in ghee and builds a small fire. He mixes ghee with rice (or barley and sesame seeds). Prayers are said while the rice is passed through the congregation. When the priest says svaha, a syllable offering oblations, after each prayer is completed, the devotees throw the grains into the fire and the priest spoons in the ghee causing the fire to flare up very dramatically. More prayers are said responsively, including the svaha, and the priest keeps adding wood to the fire to keep it going. Everyone stands up, and the bride and groom, holding bananas before them in their folded hands, stand by the fire while the prayers continue. The bananas are now placed in the fire. Everyone present chants Hare Krsna while the priest mixes ashes from the fire with the leftover ghee and a mark of ashes and ghee is placed on everyone's forehead. A large feast concludes the festivities.

The stated ideal of the membership is to marry in order to have and raise children in Krsna Consciousness. The rules of celibacy are broken for couples desiring to have children. They may have sexual relations once a month on the most auspicious day for conception. Because sex like everything else is performed for Krsna's pleasure, the couple must chant fifty rounds on their japa beads for purification before engaging in sexual activity.

In the spring of 1972, Bhaktivedanta decided to change his policies on marriage and householders cohabitating in the asrama. These changes are explained by a disciple:

> Srila Prabhupada has been troubled by many letters from the devotees saying that they and their spouses are having trouble getting along together. They always describe all of their troubles in full, including sexual problems. Some of their descriptions were very detailed and Prabhupada, being sannyasa, should not be reading that stuff. So now no grhasthas live together in the temples anymore.

Moreover, most marriages which I observed were troublesome. For one thing there is a lot of tension between a married couple which can become disruptive to the functioning of the temple. Some couples who cannot bear to be together will separate by going to different temples. A second problem is created when one of a couple is not sure of his committment to ISKCON and is considering blooping. Most of the time the prospective blooper will try to convince his (or her) spouse to bloop with him. It is fairly common to see a wife leave the movement reluctantly at the urging of the husband. It is not unusual to see one spouse leave the movement and the other to stay in it. If it is a woman who stays, the devotees will say that she is like one of the gopi girls, who left their husbands to be with Krsna.

Another problem is created by the Vedic position on women which relegates the women completely to the charge of the men. A girl is born a charge of her father, at marriage she is handed over to her husband, and later, if he dies or takes sannyasa, she becomes the responsibility of any grown sons she may have. In the American asrama the women are under the care of their godbrothers (ISKCON males) until they marry, unless their parents are ISKCON members. ISKCON women are discouraged from doing anything on their own, so they cannot even walk out of the temple without permission. If they go out to do errands, they are always accompanied by another ISKCON member. A woman who is married should ask her husband's permission to do anything beyond her prescribed temple duties. Ideally, the woman must be completely submissive and a constant servant to her husband. The American women devotees do not seem to be able to live up to the Vedic ideal for women, and this is a constant source of friction between man and wife.

It is also worthy to note that there are fewer women than men in the movement. Usually the females will comprise only about a third of the entire population of any temple.

These problems were the major factors influencing Bhaktivedanta Swami's new attitudes toward marriage and its place in the temple. He decreed that henceforth all of the women would sleep in the women's quarters and the men in the men's quarters whether married or not. The only exceptions to this rule are at New Vrndavana, ISKCON's communal farm in West Virginia, where married couples will still be householders and such temples as that in New York, where some nearby apartments are rented to be occupied only by married couples.

CHILDREN AND EDUCATION

In a letter to an expectant father, Prabhupada said, "Raising children is a great responsibility, and a prospective parent should be convinced that he can deliver his child from the clutches of birth, death, disease and old age. If that conviction is there, then there is no objection to having hundreds of children and raising them in Krsna Consciousness."

Children born into ISKCON are given a spiritual name at birth and nursed for a long period after birth, perhaps as long as two years. Sometimes a male child will have an annaprasana ceremony, when he gets his first tooth. A *Srimad-Bhagavatam* and some coins are put before the baby for him to choose between. Whatever object the child chooses first is believed to determine whether the boy will be spiritually or materially inclined in his future life. This ceremony is not mandatory and is performed only if the child's parents desire it.

Until the age of five a child is constantly cared for by his mother in whatever temple she happens to live. Other women help her out with some of her child care duties, and at times the children are collectively cared for in order to free the mothers for work. Many mothers take their children out on the streets for san-kirtana almost every day, and many of the children love it. "Prabhupada has told the devotees that children should do as they please until age five. They should not be stopped from doing anything," one mother explained. A very mischievous boy of three and a half was observed in the Amsterdam temple. The devotees pitched in to give him small errands and tasks to do to keep him busy. He was given a pot and told to go around and serve out seconds of lunch prasada to everyone who wanted it, and he served it out with his hands regardless of whether people were ready for seconds. The pot was large and he was stumbling all over. In general, this child was very difficult to control and was only reprimanded when he headed toward the altar in the temple to crawl onto it. He ran around hitting people and grabbing their things whenever possible. Much of the time he was ignored until it became absolutely impossible to ignore him any longer.

Other children were observed behaving similarly, and some visitors have pointed out that the devotees offered them little or no attention and affection. Some of the children are very carefully attended by their mothers, and these children appear less troublesome and more serene. A visitor described his experiences this way:

> After lunch I went back to the basement for a while to help out, but first I played a little with the small children who seemed to be craving for attention. When I withdrew, the children tried to get attention from other passers-by, who just shoved them aside. I guess I also expected the mothers to cast me a smile upon seeing me play with their children. But there was none of that and it disturbed me somewhat.

Some women devotees got into a discussion of Prabhupada's mother after one of them quoted Prabhupada as having said that his mother would be so glad if she could see him alive today. The others discussed what this statement could mean, and the woman answered, "Prabhupada's mother was constantly doing things to keep him alive. Every mother wants her children to live and be better than she was." She hugged her child and said, "Nandeeni will be a one thousand times better devotee than I am."

Carol, a girl of eight whose father is a devotee, was assigned to a young woman devotee entrusted to be her guardian. The guardian, who had no children of her own, was very confident of her child-raising abilities. They went to the Boston temple, where for a couple of months Carol did not attend any school or classes at all. The guardian presented the ISKCON view of child rearing:

> I am in complete charge of Carol. Carol's mother is in a mental institution and her father is in the New York temple learning Krsna Consciousness, so I have been given responsibility for Carol. I purposely took her away from the New York temple, where there are fifteen kids and they have a school. She needed to be taken away from the influence of the other kids to try to further her Krsna Consciousness, because she can be a wild child. She should begin to use her intelligence and reason or she will let her senses run wild because she is so conditioned materially.
>
> At the age of five children will be broken away from their parents and sent to the ISKCON school. In Vedic culture the parent gives the child lots of love and whatever he wants until age five. From five to eight, we begin to teach discipline and educate them. At age eight through sixteen, the parent becomes like a lion to the child in order to teach him. This is a difficult time because of adolescence and the parents must be very strict. At age sixteen, the parent is no longer a lion, but becomes a friend. There is no question of separation—if a child wants to go out and get a job the parent lets the child go. At age sixteen, children can choose to continue in Krsna Consciousness, get a job or continue their education.
>
> The main object in taking care of a child Carol's age is to make sure she does not engage in any nonsense activities, to cultivate her mind in Krsna Conscious-

ness. She plays outside for exercise—sometimes she plays that she gets a boat and goes to India to see Srila Prabhupada.

The city is not good for bringing up children. The school will eventually be in New Vrndavana, West Virginia, where the kids can play with cows, pick berries, and play the pastimes of Krsna.

At this point Carol broke in and said she did not like the warm milk but likes cold milk. Her guardian replied

"What does Krsna like?"
Carol answered, "Warm milk, Prabhupada likes warm milk."
The guardian said, "That's right—we take what Krsna gives us—we don't try to please our senses."
The pujari interrupted, "Carol, will you please go out to the shed in the yard for cow dung for Tulasi Devi?"
Carol said, "That's pure, right?"
"Yes," said the pujari.

There are a few young teen-agers in the movement. One boy of twelve asked his parents if he could become a devotee in the Washington, D.C., temple. After two years as a devotee, he asked if they would send him to ISKCON's school, Gurukula, which they allowed. A fifteen-year-old girl who had been asked to leave another temple came to the Boston temple, where, after a week, she was asked to leave. When she was asked why she quit high school to join ISKCON instead of finishing her studies while remaining a devotee, she replied, "School—that's nonsense! I don't need it; I'm going to have a husband soon and my whole life will be in a temple." Some devotees asked this girl why she does not go to Gurukula. The girl was quite emphatically negative on this subject, and claimed that all the fifteen-year-old girls were supposed to do there was to mop floors and that under no circumstances would she subject herself to that. This girl always kept in close touch with her mother, who finances all the bus trips from temple to temple. When last seen, the girl was on her way to the New York temple.

Other older children have some trouble adjusting to temple life, especially some of the children of people who became members of ISKCON late in life. The devotees say that they are "just too deep into sense gratification and materially conditioned." One boy was left at the New Vrndavana farm along with two other siblings while his mother traveled with the road show. While in the charge of the devotees, he ran away. When the devotees informed his mother that her fifteen-year-old son had "split," she shrugged it off and said, "I guess he'll just have to get kicked around a lot in karmi life before he comes back and realizes where his real life is."

In 1971, a primary school, Gurukula, was started in Dallas, Texas, based on the convictions that all the suffering of humanity is due only to ignorance; giving young people the knowledge to end the suffering condition of life is to perform the highest form of welfare work; and the suffering of children is the direct effect of their karma from past lives. By 1974 there were ninety-eight children and forty-nine adults at the school. Tuition and room and board are one hundred dollars a month for those who can pay; those who cannot are subsidized by their home asramas, by donations, or through profits from the Spiritual Sky Incense Company.

The devotees point out the Vedic scriptures which state that without spiritual education, a human being is no more than a polished beast, even if he has university degrees or great wealth and prestige. Nonsectarian spiritual knowledge, based on authentic scriptures, is not being taught in today's schools and universities; therefore, the need for instruction in spiritual science must be filled by Gurukula. Bhaktivedanta Swami wrote a letter to his devotees advising, "The old system of Gurukula should be revived as a perfect example of a school designed to produce great men; sober and responsible leaders who know the real welfare of the citizens."

The word Gurukula means the place of the spiritual master. Young children are taught Sanskrit, English, geography, history, and the bare rudiments of mathematics, starting at age five. Pupils are divided into three age levels and are separated according to sex in the oldest or advanced group. The girls are instructed in cooking and sewing. All children are taught in accordance with the state of Texas requirements for elementary school education up to the sixth grade. The academic subjects are taught in the context of Krsna Consciousness, reading from specially prepared books on such subjects as the pastimes of Krsna. The daily round of activity is the same as that of any temple in the movement.

Gurukula teachers are strict and soft-spoken. By Texas standards none are qualified; but state education officials have no jurisdiction over private schools, and the teachers are chosen by the headmaster. The teachers admit that their teaching methods may be old-fashioned but that they reflect the aim of the school: to teach self-control.

The children chant and dance a great deal. "It is a great release. Life here is very exacting," explains a teacher. "Instead of stifling or perverting emotion, we let it out by chanting and dancing." Learning exercises are also chanted.

The children board at the school separated from their parents, although visiting is allowed. Each teacher has charge of a small group of children. He or she lives in full-time association with them, caring for and educating them in the basics of academics and Krsna Consciousness. The teachers are authorized, ordained clergy of ISKCON, and all personally follow regulative practices of the society. Therefore, they claim to teach by example in the Vedic tradition, not merely by verbal precepts, because verbal precepts are thought to be worthless without practical examples. The children are disciplined affectionately, so that they will "naturally" develop a taste for spiritual, devotional life. In this way, ISKCON hopes that they will come to realize, quite spontaneously, that serving spiritual objectives in life and "developing pure love of God is great fun and the real fulfillment of life's sojourn."

The devotees believe that the educational institutions of the United States produce "hippies, malcontents, and misfits," and that much of youth rejects education geared merely toward material gain because it gives no real satisfaction. Furthermore, these youths are losing all interest in education, and want only to enjoy life irresponsibly. This nation is prosperous, but if the future generations are not interested in assuming responsible leadership, then the country's future is not bright. Despite all material prosperity, young people today are confused and frustrated. The teachers at Gurukula see themselves as giving practical instruction, starting at an early age, on how one can live perfectly in the material world engaged in devotional service, thus fulfilling all one's desires in this life and the next. This alone is supposed to create peace and harmony within the individual self and in society. A female devotee summed it up very well when she told the researcher, "A little reading, a little writing, and a lot of love of God will be all my kid needs."

6 / I am not this body

I offer my humble obeisances unto His Divine Grace Prabhupada A. C. Bhaktivedanta Swami . . .
whose vibrations caught the ears of young psychedelic middle-class renegades
   searching for alternatives to their legacy of lies and materialism,
who chanted and danced in a ring with longhair boys, girls, beads, beards, and
   headbands below the shadow of Hippie Hill in Golden Gate Park on bright
   March and April afternoons,
who lectured a thousand Hell's Angels, hippies, and teenie-boppers in the strobe-
   flashing Avalon ballroom on the glories of Lord Caitanya's sankirtan movement and, hands upraised, danced with poet Ginsberg, Moby Grape, Grateful
   Dead and Big Brother to Hare Krsna, Hare Krsna, Hare Krsna, as Tim Leary
   looked on benevolently. (Hayagriva dasa Adhikari)

The Hare Krsna devotees believe that identifying with one's material body
is one of the greatest pitfalls of the human form of life. The body is a vehicle for
going back to Godhead; therefore, the devotees are advised to treat it as such. The
human form of the body is made for regulation, not like animals, who are made for
unrestricted sense pleasures. Material life is considered a disease, and this material
body is a symptom of one's diseased form of life. Controlling one's senses and
bodily desires will help one to self-realization. The prayer said aloud in English by
the devotees before every meal makes this position clear:

> This material body is a lump of ignorance, the senses are a network of paths
> leading to death. Of all the senses the tongue is the hardest to control. It is very
> difficult to control the tongue in this world. You Lord Krsna are so kind to us—
> you have sent us this very nice prasadam just to control the tongue. We take this
> prasadam to our full satisfaction. We glorify your Lordships Sri Sri Rhada and
> Krsna and in love we call for Lord Caitanya and Prabhu Nityananda to please
> help us.

Devotees, whose life histories form the major substance of this chapter, have
little regard for their bodies which are, after all, only material. "The cause of
suffering is from spiritual rather than physical malnutrition," say the devotees,
whose emphasis is on giving instruction on the philosophy and practice of bhakti
yoga, which are considered by them to be the highest form of welfare work. The
resultant effect is minimal attention to bodily maintenance, and this only because
the body is used in the service of Krsna. Extreme cleanliness is taught by Prabhupada, but little attention is given to clothing, make-up, or personal accoutrements.

A female devotee.

The devotees point out the practical aspects of a shaved head, how clean it is, and how cheap and easy to maintain are the dhotis and saris worn by the members of ISKCON.

The ISKCON temple can be viewed as a forcing house for changing people as Goffman (1961: 12) suggests, where the devotees consciously set out to change both their personal and social identities. In order to bring these changes about, a devotee voluntarily subjects himself to a series of abasements, degradations, and profanations of his self. The alienation from his society, from his family and friends begins before an individual becomes a devotee, but entrance into the temple is a formal recognition of this alienation and tends to reinforce it. The devotee's former life is relegated to the status of a dream as Bhaktivedanta Swami (1970a: 13) cautions his devotees:

> These bodily activities are in the sleeping stage. Just as we see dreams in the sleeping stage, similarly, all these bodily activities are dreams. Just think for yourself—how many incidents have there been in your past life? If you think of them they will appear just like dreams. At least for myself this is the case. I was born in India, educated, then married, then I had very good days with my wife, got some children, some of whom died some of whom are living, some of whom are married and have begotten children. All this occurred in my past life. Now it is all a dream. I have no connection with it.

The task of remodeling himself becomes all important for the new devotee. The identity of the new devotee is directly attacked by the deprivation of the paraphernalia of his prior status and self-concept as he seeks to redefine his identity. The most obvious degradation a devotee must endure is the appearance change to which he finds himself committed. For many of the men shaving beards, mustaches, and their usually long hair can be quite traumatic, so many devotees procrastinate "shaving up" until social pressure is brought to bear. One devotee said of her husband who had not "shaved up" after several months as a full-time devotee, "He is surrendering to Krsna hair by hair—it is that difficult." Each devotee immediately adopts the yellow or saffron "uniform" and marks the body with tilaka. The men wear their remaining hair in a sikha and the women must braid their hair. Many of the women wear rings in their ears and nose. Some devotees consider the nose ring to be symbolically similar to the nose rings used for cattle. The women must also have their heads covered in the temple, and all devotees are required to bathe before touching the temple deity images.

These are physical changes, outward signs which the devotees use to mark themselves off from the larger population to make it easy for people to recognize them on the streets as devotees. The strange clothing and hair styles gain attention and fulfill a function of changing a person's social identity from hippie, office worker, student, construction worker, or whatever the person was in his former life. So deep are the changes that most devotees do not wish to discuss their former lives at all, and the average devotee has to be pressed to reveal any facts of his former life.

New recruits entering ISKCON either give all of their property to the movement or distribute it among friends. All property within the temple is not personally owned, but communally owned. With the exception of Bhaktivedanta Swami's books, a pair of shoes, japa beads, a sleeping bag, and a few items of jewelry, the devotee is stripped of his possessions. Many items of clothing are communally owned. Laundry is placed in bins, which in the men's room are designated by such categories as Krsna's underwear, Krsna's shirts, Krsna's dhotis, and so on. In addition, each devotee is urged to give up something he loves to the deities. The devotees who cling to some remnants of private property are eventually wheedled out of these items. A woman devotee said, "Even Vasudeva Swami comes up and asks me for things. For instance, today a brahmacari who had seen my nice alarm clock came in and wanted to borrow it because his is old and doesn't work right. Whatever you have gradually becomes taken over by the other devotees."

A blooper, who returns weekly to the temple for the Sunday feast, explained his problems with the ISKCON notions of property. "I was in the temple for a couple of weeks when the devotees wanted me to hand over my bank account. Well, I was not so sure if the time was right for me to become a devotee, and when they wanted all my money I realized that I wasn't ready yet. I couldn't give up all my money because then I wouldn't have anything to fall back on if I quit."

It is extremely rare to hear any dissention about property. Once in a while a devotee may become miffed about the disappearance of his favorite shoes, but there are few items of personal property important enough to squabble about. If a devotee sees an item lying around the temple, he feels free to pick it up and use it. Most of the clothing and items used by the devotees are shabby, old, and much used; possessions seem very unimportant. This stripping of personal possessions together with the mandatory appearance alterations divest a person of what Goffman (1961: 20) calls his "identity kit." They drastically alter his sense of self and curtail his presentation of his former image to others. In addition, the individual becomes totally dependent on the temple to provide the basic necessities of existence, and is even reduced to begging on the street for laksmi.

There is a tendency among devotees to want to disregard their bodies because they feel that it is the body that entraps the devotee and is the obstacle to reaching self-realization. As Bhaktivedanta Swami has stated in one of his lectures:

> We are not meant to undergo suffering, but we are suffering because we are trapped in the material world and identifying with material bodies. Real happiness can be found if we know where to find it. Real happiness can be found in the spiritual world where there is pure unalloyed bliss with no trace of suffering, but as long as we are attached to the temporary pleasures of the material body we are in a prison. We should be working towards getting free and entering into the real life that awaits us outside the prison boundaries.

The body is the cause of all suffering and misery and a source of great annoyance in that it must be cared for at all. Under these circumstances, humility comes more easily.

The devotees readily admit that they are fallen (in maya) and that they are helpless unless they can seek a spiritual master. The complete surrender to Prabhupada and to Krsna is evidenced in the statement that "we are very, very small and can do nothing for ourselves, but must be completely dependent on Krsna for everything." Prostration before the deities and Prabhupada are symbolic of these feelings and of the humility that a devotee should always feel. For these reasons a devotee should be thinking, working, eating, dreaming, and speaking of only Krsna for twenty-four hours daily. All devotees make an effort to speak only of the glories of Krsna and repeat the sayings of their spiritual master. In addition to these signs of surrender, the devotees sleep on the floor and "take" only four to six hours of sleep at night, are advised to bathe three times a day, are allowed to eat only prasada, schedule their entire day around the needs and care of the deities, drink the bath water of the deities, wear only certain colors before the deities, must always be happy before the deities, eat food fallen to the floor, observe fasts, and serve the feet of the deities and spiritual master by constantly taking orders.

The very act of putting one's body in a humiliating position while uttering obeisances is a further assault on the self. Upon entering the temple, or in the presence of high personages, or before eating, the devotee prostrates himself on the floor, pavement, or dirt, and utters his obeisances in Sanskrit:

nama om visnu-padaya Krsna-presthaya bhatale srimate bhaktivedanta-svamin
iti namine.
I offer my humble obeisances unto his Divine Grace A. C. Bhaktivedanta Swami,
who is very dear to Lord Krsna, having taken shelter at His lotus feet.

These assaults on the self which constitute degradation rituals reinforce the
belief of a devotee that he is the most fallen, impure creature existing. For this
reason he deprives himself of all possessions, renounces everything, and even claims
to know nothing. It is Bhaktivedanta Swami who has ultimate wisdom; he knows
the route to purification. Devotees are in such a fallen state that their entire lives
must become tapasya (penance, austerity). A former devotee (blooper) believes
that the devotees are rejecting the mind's ability to think. While she was in the
movement and was attending *Gita* classes, she would look around at the devotees
sitting in the temple chanting japa silently and listening to the lecture, and all she
could think of was Orwell's novel *1984*. When she was in the Philadelphia temple
where Prabhupada's lectures are played over the loud-speaker system for twenty-
four hours a day, she was unable to sleep. This blooper felt that in the ISKCON
movement "there was a rejection of the individual ego and an assumption of a
community ego. The needs, desires, and knowledge of all individuals were subjected
to service of Krsna, not even for the good of the community."

The invasion of privacy in temple life is complete and all-pervasive. The devotees are instructed in detailed bathroom habits. They are not allowed the use of
toilet paper, but are required to take a shower after passing stool. There is no
personal privacy, and all bathing and bathroom facilities are open, but segregated
by sex. All sleeping rooms are shared, eating is communal, almost all activities are
group activities.

Devotees are supposed to find all joy in the performance of bhakti, and for this
reason all devotees aim to control feelings of anger and other personal emotions.
A good devotee should always feel happy, so all devotees attempt to eradicate all
moodiness completely. Anger is rarely expressed. When an Indian man yelled
viciously at some devotees about their treatment of him, they expressed no feelings,
but everyone present began chanting "Hare Krsna, Hare Krsna . . ." aloud. A good
devotee following the great acaryas is instructed to exhibit these personal qualities:

Kind to everyone	Meek
Never quarrelsome	Steady
Fixed in the Absolute Truth	Self-controlled
Equal to everyone	Never eats more than required
Faultless	Sane
Charitable	Respectful
Mild	Humble
Clean	Grave
Simple	Compassionate
Benevolent	Friendly
Peaceful	Poetic
Completely attached to Krsna	Expert
Nonmaterialistic	Silent

Great stress is placed on the fallen, impure condition of the devotees which
causes their sufferings in this life. Assaults on the self, in the form of degradation
and mortification of the self, are invited because of these beliefs. The bodily self is
relegated to an inferior, unclean status. A devotee strives to realize his identity as

the spiritual self within the body. To be surrendered is to see one's self as a pure spiritual soul and give one's self fully to Krsna, the Supreme Soul. One surrenders desires, thoughts, and actions to Krsna so that one's own will becomes completely dovetailed with Krsna's, at least for those moments. These are the exceptional moments, the experience of grace; for, on the whole, failure is the rule. The effort is to love God through Prabhupada from the point of failure, because the love of God is extraordinarily difficult. This path of love of God is a brutal revelation to the devotee that he cannot achieve his goals. Following the desires is the path of least resistance; the path of illusion. The purification of the spirit-soul requires a constant vigil over thoughts, actions, and speech. When a devotee has thoughts of anger, lust, or greed, and can refrain from expressing them, it is a very great achievement. A devotee must be prepared to give his entire self to lead a life of day to day obedience and service. The devotee faces a constant struggle to maintain his attitude of bhakti by subjecting himself to degradations and assaults on his identity which are designed to detach him from his former self-concept.

Van Gennep (1960) defined "rites of passage" as having three phases: the first phase comprises symbolic behavior signifying the separation of the individual from an earlier position in the social structure. The next stage is transitional or liminal, where the characteristics of the individual are ambiguous. The last stage is one of reincorporation, where the passage is completed. As they apply to ISKCON the stages are: First, entrance into an ISKCON temple, where an individual is stripped of his former identity, both personal and social. Second, the liminal stage, the "betwixt and between," when the devotees are at the neophyte stage, and "elude the network of classifications that normally locate states and positions in cultural space" (Turner 1969: 95). They have anonymity, no status or property, and their behavior must be humble while their identity is refashioned to enable them to cope with their new station in life. These persons are considered less purified until they are initiated and receive their spiritual name. Before this ceremony these devotees are restricted due to their polluting qualities and cannot perform certain activities, such as operating the stove and cooking. Reincorporation of the harer-nama ceremony takes place after an individual has been a devotee for six months or more. At this time he makes a lifetime commitment, and receives a new spiritual name and insignia. The devotees are aware of and discuss the effects of this ceremony upon the person who undergoes it. "A person really changes when he is initiated and gets his new name. I almost didn't recognize my own husband, he had changed so much," said a young woman. The process of stripping, leveling, and purifying the person to be initiated so that he can take his place in the community of ISKCON is believed to alter his identity in readiness to take on his new identity as a servant of the Lord.

THE DEVOTEES

Who are the people who join ISKCON? What personal experiences have brought them to the point of wanting to change themselves and the nature of their life? We will now take a close look at some of the life experiences of a group of devotees and bloopers.

The first life history that is to be examined is Vasudeva, an important ISKCON swami. At the close of a long interview and taping session with Vasudeva, the researcher was stopped by a young brahmacari who was busily painting the front door of the temple. He anxiously begged me to reveal some fragments of my interview with Vasudeva. His interest was so deep and sincere that I repeated a couple of anecdotes from Vasudeva's conversation while he clung hungrily to every syllable.

When word about the interview got around the temple, the researcher was asked by other members to share the Vasudeva tapes with them. Finally, with Vasudeva's permission, I loaned the tape to those who wished to hear it. The maharaja is considered a great devotee. He is particularly distinguished for his early membership in ISKCON, for his close association with Prabhupada, for being the first man to take sannyasa in India, and for his high rank as swami. The devotees therefore wish to learn all they can from him about spiritual advancement.

Before Vasudeva came to visit this temple, I became friendly with Bodhendra, a brahmacari who had dropped in and out of the movement three times until he met Vasudeva at the New Vrndavana farm.

Until that time I was attracted to Krsna Consciousness, but it didn't seem sophisticated enough. No one else I had met so far was on the same platform as Vasudeva, and I was so impressed by him that I made my commitment. I helped Vasudeva design and paint the temple and we got so close that when he was ready to leave the temple to travel around preaching and selling incense, I volunteered to be his driver. As we traveled, people in the movement began to ask if I was maharaja's servant, and gradually I realized that Prabhupada had said that sannyasas should each have a servant and that my position was servant to Vasudeva. I was not rapid in advancement, so I was slow to realize. I did lots wrong. I was puffed up about philosophy, but maharaja was patient and kind while I learned to shave him up, massage him, get his prasada, make sure his clothes were clean and ironed, handle his correspondence, chauffeur him around, and handle his money business.

I traveled over 50,000 miles in the last year. I was with Vasudeva twenty-four hours a day and because of this I got to go on walks with Prabhupada and I even got to serve his lunch one time. After a while I got kind of separated from the movement because I never stayed in one temple like a regular brahmacari. The sannyasi was supposed to be aloof, but I took advantage of his friendship and became puffed up. Maharaja was so nice he never said anything (Prabhupada is so different, so strict with his servants, he often yells at them), and I realized that I had to work for him in a different capacity, less close. So I now travel ahead of him, preparing the way for him so that when he arrives everything goes smoothly. Maybe some day again we can regain our close relationship if I am more fixed up in Krsna Consciousness.

A short time later the researcher was fortunate enough to observe Vasudeva's visit to the temple. He is small and thin, walks with a limp, is well-spoken, and is very calm and controlled. If we happened to be conversing and food was served to him, he would hand his plate to me and wait patiently until he was served again. If someone entered the room his animated attitude would change, and he would ignore me completely to show that he was not associating with a woman.[1] It was obvious that Vasudeva's keen mind derived great pleasure from intellectual bantering, although at times he would feel compelled to resume the aloofness and silence demanded by his status. He very kindly shared his experiences with us in the biography that follows.

[1] All swamis are forbidden to associate with women.

From the beginning of his life, Vasudeva's strong belief in God permitted him to follow in his father's footsteps as a "preacher." This role model remained a patterning force in his life even after he rejected his father's religion in his younger years. He met Bhaktivedanta Swami and related to him as a strong father figure, and once again, thanks to Bhaktivedanta Swami, Vasudeva became a full-time preacher with a guaranteed following.

HIS HOLINESS VASUDEVA DASA GOSVAMI: A BIOGRAPHY

Vasudeva speaks of his childhood as though he were born into preaching. In his formative years he frequently "preached" to the neighborhood children on the subjects of God and Jesus Christ, his all-consuming interests.

Vasudeva, the son of a minister, was born thirty-four years ago in a small town north of New York City. Because of his natural inclination toward preaching and a deep belief in God, Vasudeva has always considered himself to be on the path to God.

> From age thirteen to eighteen I thought constantly about God. I took the agnostic route, doubting even the existence of a God. I began to experience pleasures called worldly, but due to lack of understanding of the super-sensory level, I could not cope with the existence of God. Because I wanted to enjoy the sensory level of consciousness, I questioned God. I believed then that if I simply do my best now, here, that must be the best.

After high school and college, Vasudeva attended graduate school to study religious history. Although he completed all requirements for his Ph.D., including his thesis, he never received the degree.

> In graduate school I began studying eastern philosophy and experimenting with drugs. Drugs made me very conscious that there was something to achieve, that there was a realm beyond the level of the senses. With drugs one may believe he is on that spiritual platform, or even think he has become God.
>
> What is it like to take an acid trip? Unless you actually take an acid trip you cannot know what it is like. It is the same with understanding the spiritual realm; unless you are there you cannot know it. Acid trips are all similar because they are all an experience of a subtle level of consciousness that is always the same. They are one and different at the same time. All your experiences have a oneness, but there are also differences. It is like going to the same theatre all the time. You may see a different movie, but you are always in the same theatre. The drugs made me aware. At that time I thought I had reached the goal, but looking back, all I gained was the awareness. This awareness led me to abandon my studies and go to India because I was disgusted, frustrated with the whole material world. Everything seemed meaningless. What is that piece of paper, that Ph.D.? By material standards it means that you are the most educated, but I knew down deep that I was not educated because I didn't know who I was or what I was doing. If you don't know who you are, how can you love anyone else? I had read of so many people who had gone to India and they found themselves.
>
> I was very much influenced at that time by Somerset Maugham's *The Razor's Edge*. Harry Barrows was a very romantic character. I identified with him and his search. In India, though, I found nothing because they were trying to get to what I was leaving behind. The young people I came in contact with in India had no knowledge of what I was searching for, or any desire for it, but they sure wanted my wristwatch!

I was not so much disillusioned as I was reminded of a book my father used to talk about in his sermons. It was called *Acres of Diamonds*, and was probably popular in the twenties or thirties. It was about a man who spent his whole life searching for diamonds all over the world and he died in the search without ever finding any diamonds. His son later sold the property that his father had owned and later it was discovered that there were acres of diamonds in the back yard. What I was thinking was that I was born in a particular part of the world probably for some good reason, and if I'm ever going to find out what is my relationship to the absolute, I'll probably find it out right back there.

After six months in India, Vasudeva returned to New York where he met Srila Prabhupada.

My friend Shankara dasa, who was my college roommate, met Prabhupada one afternoon on Houston St. Prabhupada said, "Please come in and see if this place is suitable for holding meetings." Shankara said, "Yes, that's fine." He was being kind to the old man. He came back and told me about his experience. I went to hear the old man speak before Shankara did. It was wonderful. It reminded me of an experience I had in Calcutta, which was the one thing that impressed me while I was in India. Shankara and I were sitting on the roof of the Salvation Army where we had a room. We were smoking hash in our water pipes. Suddenly I heard this ching, ching, ching, and I said to Shankara, "Let's go find that music." We went down into the alley where the music was coming from and we ran into two men who wouldn't allow us to enter the place. We returned to the roof and smoked a little more hash. I said, "I am going down again," and I went back to that place. I pushed the two men out of the way and went in. There were twenty or thirty young men and boys sitting under a tree in a courtyard of a house. They invited us to sit down. It was a most incredible experience and it . ansported me to realms I've never been in before. I was intoxicated. It was a far-out experience like a trance. I don't know how long we sat there.

When we came down to our senses, I didn't think much more about it until I met Srila Prabhupada, and then I remembered it. It suddenly occurred to me that these men were devotees. I remember the *Srimad-Bhagavatam* (*Bhagavata Purana*) sitting there in front of some of the men. Also, just before leaving Calcutta, I went to an art show and picked up a bunch of paintings there. I didn't know what they were until after I met Prabhupada and it turned out that they were paintings of Lord Caitanya, Lord Jagannatha, and devotees dancing in kirtana. Later I brought these paintings over to Srila Prabhupada who said, "You see, in your last life you were a devotee, but you do not remember. Because of your past you picked these out. Why, out of all paintings, did you pick these?" Why, of all things, did I also want to go to hear that kirtana? If you look at my life, you see this substantiated by the *Bhagavad-gita* (sixth chapter), where it refers to the man who practices this yoga, but doesn't make it all the way. Krsna says that in one's next life he immediately takes life in a very pious family or a very rich family. I took birth in a very pious family. We pick up in this life where we left off in our last life.

Initially, Vasudeva was attracted by the chanting and also by "Srila Prabhupada's wonderful voice when he was chanting the Sanskrit." He knew this was something very different, even though he did not understand very much of what Prabhupada was saying, particularly the philosophy involved. At the time Vasudeva was not worried about this.

I simply liked the vibes; the Sanskrit was like music. I just kept coming until he asked me to move into the temple. At first I did not recognize Prabhupada as the spiritual master. I was one of those LSD gurus. Actually many people used to visit our apartment and would ask me to tell them what to do, instruct them. But when I went to Prabhupada I understood I'd have to be a student before I became a master. At first I did not recognize how great he is. The realization came slowly. The first realization that he is guru came when in his presence I felt satisfied. Then I learned the process from him.

I now feel that I have fulfilled the Bible. Jesus Christ said he had one commandment, and if you fulfill that one commandment, you have fulfilled them all. This is that "thou shall love the Lord thy God with all thy heart, with all thy soul, with all thy might, and thy neighbor as thyself." If we carry out the orders of our spiritual master we fulfill all of that.

I asked Bhaktivedanta to be my spiritual master very soon after moving in with him. Actually, I wanted to serve him in some way. I saw he was living alone; he was cooking his own meals and everything. I was a pretty good cook so I said, "Swamiji (we did not call him Prabhupada in those days), would you like me to come cook for you?" He said, "Oh, yes, that would be very nice." Bhaktivedanta showed me how to cook capatis, dahl, curry, and vegetables. One day in the kitchen, I asked him to be my spiritual master. "Oh yes," he said. "Why not?" I was the first to be his disciple.

That year, Bhaktivedanta Swami became sick and traveled to Vrndavana, India, for treatment and rest. Vasudeva accompanied him and was impressed by the treatment administered by the Ayurvedic physicians.

Ayurvedic medicine is very different than western medicine which is based on needles and guess. Ayurvedic treatment is based on actual science. (It is almost lost today.) Simply by feeling the pulse, the Ayurvedic physician can tell you what are the symptoms of your experience. He does not ask you. I saw it. Then he prescribes some natural herbs or chemicals, depending on how serious the disease is. Gold or gems may be taken internally. The western system is not very perfect. It is very, very hard on the body. Actually, we have no faith in medicine men, east or west. We only have faith in Krsna.

Before they left for India, Bhaktivedanta indicated that he wanted Vasudeva to take sannyasa (the renounced order), and that it would be done in India.

There was a special fire ceremony which was very auspicious because it was done on Krsna's appearance day in that most holy temple of Vrndavana, Radha-Damodara temple, established by the Gosvamis of Lord Caitanya. At the most auspicious part of the ceremony, hundreds of people poured into the temple. They came over to where we were holding the fire sacrifice and started throwing coins and offering obeisances to me. People were saying the sannyasa looks just like Lord Caitanya. Prabhupada told me that Rupa and Jiva Gosvami were present; that their bodies were resting there; but their bodies were not material; they were not cremated or thrown to the dogs. They may rot to our vision, but actually they do not rot. For those who want to disbelieve, Krsna provides every opportunity. The usual process is for a person to be older when he takes sannyasa,[2] but in unusual circumstances one may take sannyasa when they are young. For instance, Caitanya was twenty-four. This means in his previous life Caitanya was ready or had been sannyasa. In our society, what could we do? We had no old men, so Srila Prabhupada, by his causeless mercy, advanced me to sannyasa. I did not feel inadequate for this because I was a little puffed up and that took time for Krsna to correct. I soon saw my real position as his eternal servant.

My mission as a sannyasa is to travel and to preach, so now I have started a road show. How can you get people to listen to preaching in this age of Kali?

[2] See Chapter 5, "Socialization of devotees."

You can't set up a tent and say, "Now I'm going to hold a revival meeting." So we travel with a rock band, performers, deities, and prasada to bring this religion to the people.

YASODA DEVI DASI: A BIOGRAPHY

We will now meet Yasoda, who is quiet, somewhat shy, warm, and personable. Most people are drawn to her pleasant face and soft blue eyes which come alive when she speaks of Krsna.

Yasoda seems to interact better with women than with men; her mother and, later, Stanley's mother were patterning forces in her life. Her relationships with men are all similar to the distant relationship that she experienced with her father while in her formative years. Now that she lives in an ISKCON temple she hardly associates with men at all. There are the strong father figures of Bhaktivedanta Swami and the temple president with whom Yasoda can relate to at a distance. Bhaktivedanta Swami is a vague person hardly ever seen by Yasoda, but each day she hears his lectures on tape, each day she gazes at his picture and occasionally she can write to him if she has a problem. He is, for Yasoda, a Christ figure, too lofty to be approached, but someone before whom she can prostrate herself and someone she can serve—always at a distance.

Yasoda never feels emotionally involved with the young men she meets; therefore, even her five-year relationship with Stanley was superficial. She admits that they came together out of convenience and that their sex life was the only binding factor. Never did they feel any closeness. Nor could she feel comfortable with the brahma-caris as her only associates for her first months in the movement. Therefore she left the first temple and moved to another where there were more women. The threat of closeness with men drives her to seek a temple where she can disengage herself effectively from men.

I have presented Yasoda because she is an example of a dedicated devotee who, in her self-effacing way, is a mainstay of temple life. She is almost the "average" devotee, the dependable person who exhibits obedience in action and spirit by performing all her obligatory chores no matter how dull or unimportant. Day after day she serves the deities tirelessly, without fanfare, and little, if any, attention to herself. She is fully in tune with her new identity as a devotee. Without people like Yasoda, the temples could not function. Her biography illustrates some of the ingredients necessary for becoming a successful devotee. She exhibits a deeply felt need for a God, for an ideology and a structure in which to act out these needs which "establishment" religion has not been able to provide.

Yasoda was born thirty years ago in Baltimore, Maryland. As a young child, she and her mother had a close, loving relationship. Sunday church-going and before-meal prayers were regular habits for this Presbyterian family. At home, Yasoda's mother read the Bible, prayed daily, and spoke often to her family about Christ, in whom she believed deeply. Yasoda was never able to have a close relationship with her busy executive father, whom she describes as totally businesslike about everything. He had no interest in religion, and seemed unable to show warmth or closeness. Her mother was pleased when Yasoda joined ISKCON at age twenty-seven, and takes a great interest in the movement herself. Yasoda's father, on the other hand, has absolutely no interest in the philosophy.

I've always believed that there was a God. At first he seemed to be an old man with a long white beard; a fatherly, no, a grandfatherly figure, sitting on a big throne directing everything that was going on. I used to pray frequently as a child. At twelve or thirteen years old, after I was confirmed into the church, I'd go to the Sunday evening church socials at the urging of my parents.

Yasoda was taken out of public high school and sent to a nonsectarian private girls' school. Her main interest became sports because her closest friends in the school were interested in activities such as field hockey. Yasoda participated just to go along with the crowd, not because she enjoyed it. In fact, she "got tired running up and down the field." Her true interests were in art and literature, and these continued to be her main enjoyments throughout her college years. Herman Hesse was her favorite author because she could identify with his characters and their experiences.

Yasoda describes herself as always having been frivolous. Her father used to ask her what she wanted out of life and she could only answer, "I just want to be happy." Her father would urge her to become "a responsible citizen, command respect, take obligations and fulfill them." He felt that the principle of obligation was more important than her personal feelings. Feelings should be suppressed and duties should be fulfilled at any price.

After graduating from high school, Yasoda attended a women's college in Ohio. During this time she had her "first real contact with boys." She had always been "terrified of boys" in the past, but was now able to establish a friendship with a young man named Lou. During one of their frequent discussions about God, Lou told Yasoda that he had figured out a mathematical way of disproving God's existence. She returned to her dormitory room that night feeling

> . . . horrible and completely, absolutely lost. I just knew there was a God and that everything this boy said was absolutely crazy. I had a strong feeling of the presence of God at that time.

At the end of her sophomore year, Yasoda transferred to an art school in Baltimore, but she was not really serious about her art studies and left after a year to attend a large urban university.

> There, too, I had no goal. There was nothing I was working towards. It was just the idea. I just wanted to be happy and to have fun. I wasn't learning anything. None of my professors had anything to say. I was beginning to develop a sense of wanting to know more about God, but there were no religious courses for me to take.

Yasoda graduated from college and met a boy whom she thought at the time she wanted to marry. They took a trip to Laguna Beach, California, together.

> Still something was missing in my life. I was not sure what, but I sensed that it was spiritual in nature. I had to start talking to people about it, and discovered that this boy was not even interested in knowing anything about God. I then did not want to spend the rest of my life with him. So I went back to Maryland, where I met Stanley, who I was with for five years. This boy's mother was a very devout Catholic with a strong faith in prayer and a strong personal relationship to God. I was closer to her than I had even been to my own family. I began going to Mass every Sunday, and the vacuum within me was filled a little bit, but not completely. Now I knew that the missing element in my life was definitely spiritual, and I thought about becoming a Catholic.

Later, Stanley and I went to New York City, and there I felt a sense that I needed something solidly spiritual in my life. I took some education courses at Hunter College and was also working part-time in a bank. Often, on my way home from work, I would stop into a church and just throw myself down at the foot of a statue of Christ, just wanting to feel some presence. I never thought of Christ as being God, but I needed some communication with God. It was like I was paying my obeisances to Christ, but I didn't know it at the time. It was just out of frustration that I would throw myself down. It was just this emptiness wanting to be filled. I wanted to get away to a convent or something.

About this time, Yasoda began to see Krsna devotees carrying bead bags. She became very curious about what was in them, but "was too timid to ask." She was also curious about their temple which she frequently passed, but was "afraid to enter." At this point, Stanley and Yasoda began experimenting with marijuana and hash. They also decided to move back to Maryland, where Yasoda got a job teaching nursery school. On weekends they went to visit a friend's farm.

I took mescaline there for the first time. It was very bad and I completely lost control of myself, hallucinated, and became very frightened. Everything seemed so messy, dirty, and horrible to me, but I did get a strange feeling of power. I even knew that I could walk through the walls of a nearby building if I wanted to. I guess I knew, for a moment, that I was not this body.

Yasoda's friends at the farm were vegetarians, and Yasoda soon decided to stop eating meat.

I began to think back to the trip to California I had taken, and remembered visiting a slaughterhouse in Nebraska, where I could see the suffering in the eyes of the cows. I began to think that I had no right to eat the flesh of animals, and stopped eating meat. Stanley continued eating meat and I had to fix it for him, but I wanted nothing to do with it.

Around this time, I also began to read the *Gita* and other Indian religious literature. The *Gita* was my favorite; a practical book. I wanted to live like that.

I got into the *I Ching* with two girlfriends. One day the *I Ching* predicted that we'd all be in Europe within thirty days, and it just turned out that it was exactly what happened to us.

Nothing in Yasoda's life at this time gave her any satisfaction.

I finally decided to go to Europe, even though Stanley didn't want to go with me. It was not like we were ever happy together; it was more being together out of convenience. Only our sex life bound us together. So I left for Europe with my girlfriend, Debbie, where we hitchhiked around. Everywhere we went we met young people who let us stay with them. I felt that youth was just one big happy family, but, of course, a lot of it had to do with drugs. Everyone was high all the time or taking LSD. We kept ending up in Amsterdam because the dope was so cheap there. In Copenhagen we began to chant Hare Krsna, which I had first heard in New York. When I felt stress or anxiety, I'd chant and I could feel some relief. One time we found ourselves in a Volkswagen bus with a lot of people traveling all night to Copenhagen. There was something about these people that made me feel fearful, so I chanted Hare Krsna for about two hours. When I stopped chanting aloud and lay back, I closed my eyes and could hear what sounded like a choir of angels chanting. This went on all night and I never remember feeling so wonderful. In the morning, a boy who had been on the bus said he heard my Hare Krsna chanting, and after I stopped he continued to hear the chanting all the rest of the night. The rest of our trip we always chanted, and for all that time everything was perfect. We didn't have to wait for rides. The sun was always shining.

Debbie and I began to dream of finding a forest where we could just play and not have any worries and responsibilities. We went to Switzerland to find it and that was the worst of all. The people were so cold; everyone had tight little fences, saying "This is my property—you keep off!" Besides, all the woods were full of people. Since we did not find the ideal place we went back to Amsterdam and stayed on a house-boat for seven dollars a week, until we had to go back to the U.S. because our airplane tickets were about to expire.

Yasoda went home for a while, intending to return to Europe as soon as she could sell her furniture, find a home for her cats, and "settle everything with Stanley." Yasoda told a new acquaintance how much she enjoyed chanting Hare Krsna. Her friend mentioned that there was a group of people right around the corner who chanted Hare Krsna all the time, and suggested that she visit them.

From then on I began to think a lot about visiting a temple. Finally, I went, knocked on the door, and was invited to enter. It was just like stepping into the sunshine. It was so warm and friendly. I sat down for prasada with the devotees and no one even talked to me, but I didn't care. Afterwards, the devotees invited me to go out into the street on sankirtana with them. I couldn't go then, but I left knowing that I'd go back to the temple, probably to stay.

She told Stanley of her decision, and he begged her not to go. Before this, she had always wanted him to plead with her to stay with him, and needed to feel that he loved and wanted her. Now his pleading seemed like empty words.

That night in bed I had the strong feeling that I *had* to go to the temple. I didn't have any choice; that's where I belonged. I had the feeling I'd be doomed if I didn't go. The next morning I took my toothbrush and a few things, and went to ask the temple president if I could stay.

Yasoda stayed in this temple from August 1971 to January 1972. During her stay she was close to the brahmacaris because she was the only woman in the temple. Since it was not a strict temple, she could have the boys as her friends.

We were like a very close family. They were like my friends that I was looking for all my life.

In August 1971, the entire temple went to New Vrndavana for Janmastami. Yasoda found the trip to be a very confusing experience. She could not understand what was happening there, because of the disagreements about Srila Prabhupada which were then taking place. The main argument was whether or not Srila Prabhupada was God. Yasoda did not yet understand Srila Prabhupada's identity and her relationship to him.

My head was so clouded and full of darkness from so many drugs. I was chanting with a great amount of concentration, and I was trying to hear when I was chanting. I concentrated until I knew that what I was doing was right.

At this point the tie with Stanley was not yet broken. He was working in the neighborhood of the temple and came to see her often. Yasoda left the temple for a week in January to try to convince Stanley to join ISKCON with her, but was not successful and went back alone. Because she was the only woman in the temple and was constantly seeing her old friends, she asked the temple president if she could go somewhere else. The president recommended the Boston temple. Yasoda went there shortly afterwards and has been there ever since. From the beginning she was "attracted to the deities," and after her initiation, she began caring for them. Yasoda is now the devoted pujari of the Boston temple, into whose care the temple deities have been entrusted. She discharges her responsibilities with the utmost love and commitment, and is highly respected by all of her colleagues in Krsna Consciousness for her great devotion.

DIANE: A BIOGRAPHY

Diane's complicated life history is an example of a person who cannot succeed as a devotee. At first, she finds a sanctuary in a very small ISKCON temple, where she is able to curb her drug habits and function as a devotee with the guidance of a few close friends. Her move to the Boston temple begins to bring problems because she is forced to interact with more devotees, and cannot build relationships with them. Her spiritual needs appear to be minimal, but her need for close relationships with people appears to be great. At first, she claims to have problems sleeping due to recurring bad dreams, and speaks of murder dreams, suicide dreams, and of her anxiety, which she calls "agitation." Her work begins to be affected, and her personal relationships degenerate, driving her to seek a doctor's help under the guise of needing sleeping pills. It is the move to the New York temple that brings Diane's psychological problems, and her physiological need for drugs, to a head. She cannot cope with such a large, impersonal temple, which has now grown to a membership of over one hundred and thirty. The needs that brought her to the temple were not fulfilled, and her need for a God so weak that she no longer has reason to stay on and leaves. Diane's story is representative of a person who joins ISKCON hoping to solve very serious problems which are too deep to be resolved without professional attention.

Diane, a twenty-three-year-old devotee, was the second child of an upper middle-class family of four children. Diane remembers her parents as happily married, and their home life as religiously oriented. Her mother was Jewish and her father was from an Italian Catholic background. No specific religion was followed, but a belief in God was taught to the children by their parents. Diane felt that this was an important constituent of their family life.

During a long incurable illness, Diane's mother became heavily addicted to drugs. Money was plentiful, and Diane's father kept her well supplied with the necessary narcotics. Diane was taught to help care for her mother and to give her heroin injections. At this period, Diane and her mother were deeply attached, and it was very painful for her to witness her mother's suffering. Watching her mother's agony generated so much anguish in Diane that she consented to help her mother die by an overdose that she herself would administer. Diane was later to pretend that the death was accidental, although she now admits that her mother died by "mutual agreement," and that she was in the room with her mother when she died. For Diane, the death and the events surrounding it were so "horrible and traumatic" that it took her months to recover from the deep sense of shock and grief which she experienced.

After Diane learned how to give an injection she began experimenting with heroin "just out of curiosity about how it would feel." By age thirteen, she was addicted. Diane's father knew that both she and her brother were addicted and "didn't mind." The father kept them well supplied with money for fixes, his only concern being that they not make any "connections" in his house. By this time, the focus of Diane's father's life shifted to things outside the family. He began traveling a lot on business, leaving Diane and the other children at home with the household help and plenty of money for anything they needed. When he was in town, he spent his time visiting nightclubs and running around with his many women friends. Often, Diane was allowed to accompany her father and his companions to nightclubs and was exposed to what she thought at that early age was a glamorous nightlife.

Later, Diane, who showed a talent for drawing and painting, enrolled in a Philadelphia art school. While studying art she met and married an "older man." When the marriage broke up after eight months, Diane began working as a jazz singer with a group of musicians. During the course of their travels around the country, Diane was chosen by one of the group to be his girlfriend. This man was also addicted to heroin.

From this point on, Diane's story becomes extremely jumbled and it would be impossible to sort out a chronology of events. Nevertheless, her style of life and mood remain significant.

Some time later a second musician joined with her boyfriend to form a "ménage à trois" in which they lived, got high, and shared sexual relationships. Every drug possible was tried "for kicks," so life was a constant high on smack, LSD, peace drug, mescaline, and others. At another point, Diane went to live with a famous jazz musician in order to learn more about jazz, and he taught her all the real knowledge she has of jazz singing. Her heroin addiction continued; she nearly died twice from overdoses. After a chance meeting with some ISKCON devotees on the street, Diane returned with the devotees to the New York temple for a visit, and decided to stay on permanently.

It was difficult for her to give up drugs, but she managed to "cool out" with the support and help of some of the devotees.

> I was up to three spoons of smack a day, and "going through cold" was hell. At times I still go cold and yearn for smack, but now, if I need smack, I pray to the deities and chant on my beads until the desire goes away. I was most at peace with myself, and happiest, in the Third Avenue temple because the atmosphere was so ideal, and the devotees so happy.

Since she moved to the Boston temple, Diane has had some bad personal clashes with the other brahmacarinis (unmarried women devotees) with whom she is obliged to live. Most of the day she is engaged in painting, and has good rapport with the other painters with whom she works. Diane attributes her troubles with the brahmacarinis to the fact that she feels so much older, and so much more experienced. Lately she has had trouble sleeping and has requested the temple president's permission to use sleeping pills. Some of the devotees have advised Diane that she doesn't chant enough to alleviate her troubles. They also claim that she does, in fact, fall asleep at odd hours and in odd places, such as the composing room floor.

Diane has always felt ambivalence about her status as a devotee.

> When Prabhupada was at the temple the last time he was initiating and marrying devotees, I was not yet ready in my head for this. I wanted to fade into the background so Prabhupada wouldn't notice me and tell me to become initiated. I kept very quiet and out of sight as often as possible, and he hardly noticed me.

That's how you do things in Krsna Consciousness. At one point, he did suggest that I become married in Krsna Consciousness. Once there was a brahmacari in whom I was interested, but he went to India. Right now I am against marriage because there is no one I want to marry, and I don't want to be someone's slave. I really don't like the way some of the boys here treat their wives.

Diane finally moved to New York with the press, where after a couple of months, she blooped. The devotees say that she is in terrible shape, and that they saw her on the street working as a prostitute.

YVONNE AND JANARDANA DASA ADHIKARI:
AN AUTOBIOGRAPHY

We have examined three life histories that illustrate the helter-skelter value disorientation of contemporary youth that leads them to join Krsna Consciousness. Now we will take a deeper look at another life history as it is told to us by Yvonne. Yvonne is able to share her innermost thoughts and feelings about her life experiences. She describes events, people, and participation that I have described from the outsider's point of view. This points up the interaction between psychological problems and disorientation that lead youth into a state of alienation, ultimately causing them to reject the values of American society, and to seek a more satisfying ideology. Through Yvonne we will view the life of her husband, Janardana, which will further our understanding of the limitations and opportunities presented by an individual's life history for new definitions. Both Yvonne and Janardana are disoriented and alienated. They are lost in mistrust, doubt, guilt, identity confusion, isolation, despair, and are stagnating in self-absorption while longing for trust, autonomy, initiative, identity, intimacy, and integrity. We see how some of the basic conflicts of their childhoods live on in some form in their lives, and how society fails to provide the positive models, identifications, and ideology toward which Yvonne and Janardana strive.

Yvonne never learned to trust. Before she and Janardana joined ISKCON she was constantly in fear of Janardana's trying to "brainwash" her, and of the "conditioning through LSD and sex" that she believed he was doing to her. She could never quite break with him; she wanted to leave him, but followed him into ISKCON in hopes that it would save their relationship and provide a "beautiful" way of life. She never really believed in the philosophy, but wanted the feeling of community and love that she saw between the godbrothers and godsisters. She had a need for a God and was able to "get high" on the chanting, dancing, and ritual. Although Yvonne wanted the companionship and approval of the devotees, she was not willing to put up with the regimentation, and rebelled once again as she so often had in the past.

The love and admiration which Yvonne felt for her father was returned in a disappointing way. Yvonne wanted to follow in his footsteps, to be like him, but because she was a girl, her father wouldn't allow this and relegated her to a role which he considered more appropriate for a woman. Yvonne feared losing her father's love and either complied with his wishes or hid the truth from him when she could not live up to his expectations. In her relationship to Janardana she acts out many of the ambivalences which existed in her relationship to her father. She is torn between subjugating herself to Janardana and rebelling against him more strongly than she would dare to do with her father.

Janardana, on the other hand, seems to be seeking the ideology and structured setting of the temple. He is able to channel all of his energies into his transformation as a devotee, and he willingly pays the price in obedience, self-sacrifice, sickness, and hardship, if required. In ISKCON, he finds what he has been searching for, and is able to change his consciousness without the aid of drugs.

Janardana and Yvonne become locked in conflict because both aim to influence the other. He tries to make her into a devotee, while she tries to persuade him to leave the movement. Both fail after a long struggle, and each must finally accept the other for what they are. The autobiography that follows speaks for itself.

"I was brought up in a world of good away from the evils of the world," says Yvonne of her childhood in the small New Hampshire town where she was born twenty-seven years ago.

My father owned and operated a restaurant, while my mother stayed at home with me and my younger sister and brother. My mother was born a Baptist, but turned Greek Orthodox to please my father. We rarely attended church because none of us, except my father, learned enough Greek to follow the rituals and sermons.

I was a well-behaved child, and the only signs of rebellion were at the table when I refused to eat. I was very conscious of parental approval and feared losing my parents' favor, so I learned to follow their every command. Still, I was spanked for minor things more frequently than the others, and learned to fear the punishments of my mother. My father was more lenient. I did well in school, but often refused to do assigned work that I felt was useless. I was always favored enough by my teachers to get away with this. I daydreamed a lot and spent a lot of time outdoors communing with nature. I believed in a higher force than man because it was obvious to me that man could not create a tree, the sky, or the earth. One day I thought I saw God in the sky on a cloud. These feelings were personal and private, and I kept them hidden from the rest of the family fearing their disapproval and laughter. Between daydreaming and reading a lot, I lived in a world all my own.

In the sixth grade I learned of "the bomb," and lived in fear of the world's demise. I watched the political situation carefully and discussed it with my father; my mother and sister were not interested in such things.

As a teenager I was not allowed to date, but at fifteen I learned that since I was in a woman's body I would not be free, but would be passed on from my family to my future husband's authority. I discovered that my godparents had arranged the marriage of their son. What hope did I have for freedom except to avoid men and not marry?

At age fifteen I began to work for my father as cashier and hostess in his restaurant. At first, I hated the work. I feared the public contact, and cried for days on end, even in the restaurant. My father would not change his mind, and I could do nothing but accept his power over me. Later I became close to my father and looked down on other girls, thinking them to be stupid and two-faced. I felt I was better than they because I dealt with the business world now, and loved it. In my senior year of high school, I was shocked when my father sold the restaurant. I expected to take over his place and follow in his footsteps. He laughed at me, a mere girl, making me ever more aware of my subservient position as a female. So I renewed my vow never to marry. My freedom was all important to me, but my father decided that I should attend teacher's college when I graduated from high school.

At college, I still lived by my parents' rules and regulations, afraid to change even at the urging of my new college friends. I had been taught that good girls don't smoke, drink, or go out with boys. At college all the girls did these things and were good and likeable people. My friends tried to help me change, but I was afraid to. I learned about sex and babies from a college health book. During the second semester, my roommate was a lesbian. I did not dare to mention this to my parents with their Victorian principles, although by then, I wanted to leave school. I no longer wanted to teach, but to do social work and try to make the world a better place to live in. My father refused to allow me to change schools or my major. I contemplated running away to Canada, but couldn't do this because of my love for my family. I was not happy at school and attended only the classes that interested me until I finally flunked out.

At the end of my second year I got drunk and was raped. I now had another thing to hide from my parents. I took to my bed in guilt and in fear of them marrying me off, since I'd failed in school. My father was furious and considered me stupid. That summer I went to work for my godfather at the beach, enjoying myself in the sun and dating boys, but since I had no knowledge of contraceptives, I ended up pregnant. When I finally told my mother, she banished me from the house, forcing me to move in with some friends. After a while my mother intervened and sent me to a home for unwed mothers in Boston. When the baby was born, I gave it up for adoption, and was accepted back into the family, with only my mother knowing the truth about my absence. Naturally, I promised never to do such a thing again and to avoid boys, but I had been awakened sexually. I wanted my freedom, and after six months, I returned to Boston to live and work.

I had lived in Boston for three years when the hippie movement became popular. Before this I experimented with grass, but experienced no high. Then, one day, someone gave me a tab of LSD, telling me it was mescaline. I was high for a long time and before I came down, I began to see how conditioned I had been by my parents and society. I decided to leave home forever; to travel out west and to experience life and complete freedom. But on the day I was supposed to leave, I met a man named Chuck Jones. I decided not to go west because I was fascinated with this hippie and how he got that way.

Chuck, whose father was a military officer, was born in 1944 in a small midwestern town, the eldest of three children. As a child he had a terrible temper and was very hard to control. The family moved every six months all over the U.S. and Europe, and he changed schools as often. He was an erratic student, who was rebellious in school, wrote on desks, and developed a lisp due to nerves.

Religion was unimportant to Chuck's family. They were into the military social life and drinking. He was not very close to them and looked down on his sister as a person less than himself because she was a girl. In the eighth grade he ran away from the family's western home and survived for ten days in the desert on his own. Then the family moved north, and he signed up for the college preparatory course in high school. He began to date, played sports, and was well known and liked by his classmates. High school was a happy time for him.

Chuck chose a college in the South near his maternal grandparents' home, to study electrical engineering. He was given a car and a boat of his own. By now his goal in life was to become a millionaire. Chuck became successful in a summer job at a Boston cable and wire plant. As manager of the plant he was given great independence and was able to save his boss a lot of money by devising some new methods of production.

Chuck suddenly quit school in his third year. Soon after this, he broke with his family after a furious fight with his father. Chuck wanted a motorcycle and his father argued that he did not want a greaser for a son. Chuck put his fist through a wall during the fight, and went ahead and bought the motorcycle in spite of his father's wishes. After this, his only ally in the family was his grandmother.

While in college, Chuck had a preacher roommate with whom he had violent arguments and fistfights. One day as Chuck was denouncing the existence of God, a bolt of lightning struck the building which caused a crucifix to fall off the wall, and he began wondering about God. This concern about God increased after a close brush with death during sky diving, when his parachute did not open. Then, a woman acquaintance took him to a Holy Roller church where the emotion scared him, and he began to believe that religious people were crazy.

When Chuck finally quit school, he moved to Boston to work at his summer job full-time. Within a short time, his boss was killed in an airplane accident. The new management would not allow him the freedom that his former boss had given him, so he quit his job.

One night, Chuck got drunk and was assaulted by a homosexual. This was his first sexual experience, and he was in such terror of it happening again that he moved into a tough section of the city. There he was beaten up by a group of ruffians and bought a shotgun for self-protection. The same group threatened to steal his motorcycle. He reported this to the police, but they were unresponsive. He then decided to take the law into his own hands and settle the matter himself. When they returned to steal the bike, he shot the leader of the gang in the stomach, wounding him badly. Chuck turned himself in, and after a year was brought to trial. He appeared in court in a suitcoat and short hair, for the last time in his life. During the three-day trial, he aroused the anger of the judge and they argued, but there was one black man on the jury who, Chuck says, swayed the vote in favor of his freedom. At the end of the trial, the judge lectured Chuck saying, "Jones, you are a lucky man. You are insane and you should be imprisoned for ten years." Chuck now hated this country; its courts, its police—everything.

During the wait for his trial to come up, Chuck had met street people. Many of these new acquaintances had been in reform schools. They took drugs, carried guns, and committed crimes to support their way of life. He learned about the way of the street and how to protect himself better. Because he was so poor, he lived for a whole month on macaroni, until he learned how to "rip off" a phone. This became his livelihood, although he wanted no part of holdups or hard drugs. In a year's time, he had grown his hair long, started wearing jeans, and had become a member of the counter culture.

Around this time Chuck's first army induction notice was mailed. The notice never reached him because he hadn't reported his change of address. He sometimes worked as a surveyor during this period, but was more into taking LSD and smoking grass regularly. At the sight of a police uniform he would yell "pig." He got into many fights with the police, but had enough luck never to get arrested.

Eric and Amy, a young couple, invited Chuck to move in with them to share their LSD weekends. After some time, Eric turned strange, treated Amy very badly, and took up the odd hobby of breeding male fish and flushing the females down the toilet. He spent the rest of his time making three-foot square candles. The three of them stayed high constantly, but when Chuck could no longer take this insanity, he moved to a room in the center of the city. By then he was twenty-four years old and was dividing his time between dates with two teenage girls, work as a surveyor, dealing grass, listening to records, and getting high. Then he met me. That's when he stopped work and began to live with me.

I was in love and happy with Chuck for one month. We went out to eat, went to the movies, and were happy together. I was ripe for turning into a hippie and he was ripe for believing in God. It appeared to be a good match. LSD had opened me up to the conditioning of my parents and society, and to the hypocrisy of it all. The country was in a mess; close to revolution. LSD had opened Chuck up to the concept of God and a higher force in nature.

Little did I know he was conditioning me to be the person he wanted me to be. He started by giving me LSD in small doses. Since I wanted to stay with him, I accepted his authority and stopped fighting with him. He had thrown me out twice, only to repent and change his mind. We both felt sorry for each other and hoped to be able to change things and make each other a happy person.

Meantime, Chuck discovered that the F.B.I. was looking for him on a charge of draft evasion, so he decided to go into hiding. Taking me with him, he moved to the black section of town. He made a living by dealing grass, LSD, and downers. The police became the enemy. It was a real-life game of cops and robbers. Our LSD trips were carefully planned according to the instructions of one Timothy Leary. We aimed for "the clear light of peace within," since there was no peace in the world of the ghetto and outside, but only paranoia and quarrels.

I became pregnant. Chuck was delighted, but the rumors of LSD freak babies haunted me. I finally miscarried and it was never discussed again. I began taking the pill. We wanted no more children, and besides, Chuck had no intention of leaving the country for Canada to make a place of safety for me and our future children.

After the miscarriage, the relationship changed, and this was compounded when we started sharing an apartment with other hippies who ran out on the rent and stole our food. Chuck refused to face responsibility and deal with it. I was forced to. He issued orders and I carried them out. He decided that he wanted me to work. I refused and there was a bitter quarrel. Finally, I relented and got a job. Though I was working too, Chuck insisted on handling all the money and refused to give me any money at all. At first he would not allow me to buy food. When he finally trusted me to buy food, he complained that I always spent too much, so I stole in the supermarket rather than have him complain. He had already struck me a few times when I refused to obey orders.

During this time he became ill with a strep throat. He refused my help and wouldn't see a doctor. He simply lay in bed, read the *Tibetan Book of the Dead*, and suffered feverish hallucinations. He was preparing to die, but he didn't.

He had finally conditioned me to his life style and his friends. Chuck had charisma and was admired and liked by a group of friends who followed his teachings. This was the summer of Charles Manson and conditioning through LSD and sex. Chuck had his own personal guinea pig in me.

A lot of our time was spent high on grass and LSD and sex. The police were constantly around and one day Chuck was arrested and beaten up for saying the word "pig" to the head of the narcotics bureau. Chuck went to court, but the arresting officer did not appear, so he was set free. Now, after Chuck's experiences, I had a personal reason to hate the police too.

In the fall of 1969, we moved to a one-room apartment by ourselves, hoping to become more together again, but it did not really work. I was not as responsive to his sexual advances as before, and told him to date other girls. He wouldn't do this, not for a while at least. One day while I was high I told Chuck that he was crazy and that we should seek help for him because he was becoming two people. He laughed at this, just as he laughed at my tears, and my dreams of his going to jail. He constantly fought me on the issue of moving to a place of safety for us both. I saw that he did not believe in human love, in union with God, on earth or after death.

I went home for Thanksgiving. This was my first visit home, as Chuck had not wanted me to see my parents at all. I told them that I was living with Chuck. My mother simply said that Chuck would not be allowed in her house unless we got married. I tried to explain that neither of us wanted a legal tie, but it was impossible for her to understand.

Chuck took my absence as an opportunity to be with another girl. He confessed this when I came back and immediately sensed that he had been with someone else. The LSD had made me aware of psychic phenomena and my own psychic power. Chuck brought the girl home to meet me. It was tense. I was cool on the outside and jealous and hurt on the inside. He dated the other girl for a month, but after a month of my tears and his fear that I was poisoning him, he dropped her. He told me I was the only girl he could live with.

Right after this, I took an LSD trip which affected me for months to come. I wanted to leave Chuck because he was not what I really wanted, but when I tried to go, he cried. I couldn't leave him then, so I stayed on—unhappy. On this same LSD trip Chuck read a book called *The Bhagavad-gita As It Is*, by A. C. Bhaktivedanta, which he thought made perfect sense. One chapter was on how women were not equal to men and we argued over that. Chuck's close friend, Bill, was also reading this book and was deep into eastern thought and ways of life. They became closer in this common bond while Janie, Bill's wife, and I just sat and listened to them talk. Chuck stopped eating meat, and we became vegetarians. I had already seen him pass through stages on various things, so I did not pay much attention to this book. Chuck refused to let me read it for six months, saying I was too stupid to understand. I was little more than his slave; no wonder he thought I was stupid!

At this point, life was only real for me when I was high. Often I would leave my body and so would Chuck. In this condition we could relate to one another perfectly. When we finally came down after every trip, we would either move or change our life in some way. I would usually fight him over this, but it was no use as he was becoming more and more violent if I argued with him at all. At work I'd worry about him being in a fight on the street or getting arrested. He was violent on the street. He kicked the cars in his way and shouted insults to people. We did not go out often because the world was hostile and so were we.

After the incident at Thanksgiving with Chuck and the other girl, I was afraid to go away, so at Christmas I stayed home. Chuck would not allow a tree or presents, and we tripped on orange sunshine. It was heavy because the lady next door freaked out. She screamed up and down the stairs, flushed toilets, and everyone hid in their rooms. Finally, the police came and dragged her away singing "Jingle Bells," but we were not able to rise above her commotion and trip ourselves away from what was happening to her. This time all the preparation for our trip did not help. Usually we bathed, cleaned the house, prepared fresh salads and vegetables to be eaten, and "dropped" at night to avoid such disturbances. Holidays and Sundays in Boston were also quiet and safe times to trip—usually.

Our way of life was very regimented. We rose at six, took the cat to the Fens (a park), and returned for breakfast. I went to work and Chuck stayed home to read, or do his grass business, or walk around to visit friends. At night I came home, got high, cooked supper, and got high again with him. On weekends, we cleaned the house, and on Sunday we tripped. I was getting exhausted and became prone to colds and long stays in bed. We moved again, but stayed in the new place only a month. Tripping was getting too heavy in South End rooming houses. Chuck talked of becoming a preacher and traveling with me as his wife. Instead, he decided to go on the brown rice diet. I had to learn to cook all over again, according to Yin-Yang.

Then we moved into a Cambridge apartment with two other girls, a dog, and a big yard. Chuck decided that we were not going to have sex any more, and informed me of this while coming down from an LSD trip. This trip is important because it was my last one. He decided it. I had been very ill and could only lie in bed, spaced out of my mind. My eyesight had been affected by all the LSD and I was afraid I was going blind. Chuck gave me a tab of LSD and began to listen to classical music. Somehow the music hurt my ears and I was experiencing physical pain. I simply curled up in a ball and cried, unable to control the tears. Chuck became angry at me because he had to turn the music off, but then we went to visit Bill and Janie as a kindness to me. On the way there, somehow I lost Chuck in the bus, but found him again. When we got there, Bill was also tripping, but Janie was not high. Chuck and Bill started talking about a farm in

Vermont, tripping and living a life style as the swami (Bhaktivedanta) had outlined in his book. Right away it seemed like a good idea. Of course, we would all have to get married. That had me worried, since I still did not want to be legally tied to Chuck. Also I wondered who would be doing the farming with those two tripping all the time. It was when we got home that Chuck told me about no sex and announced that I would never have to work again.

In time the two girls moved out of our apartment and some other friends moved in with us. Chuck laid down the rules for the house, such as no meat eating, and no hard drugs (meaning heroin and speed), so the friends soon moved. Like so many of our other friends, these people had now gone from LSD and grass to heroin. By June we had the whole apartment to ourselves. I had quit work and Chuck had stopped me from tripping, although he did not stop himself. He wanted me to read the *Bhagavad-gita*, now that he was reading the other Krsna material and talking to the devotees on the street. This was a change from Chuck's attitude of the year before. At that time he stopped me from giving a devotee we met on the street my loose change, and always crossed the street to avoid the devotees.

The farm never materialized because Chuck and Bill could not find a farmer in Vermont to rent to them. I paid little attention to all this. It seemed impractical to me, and I went home for a week. Chuck called me back. He was tripping and one of our kittens died and he needed me to come and take it from the room. He couldn't handle it and made me throw it in the garbage since it was only a dead body and the soul had left it.

Bill and Janie joined the Krsna temple when Janie was six months pregnant. Shortly after that, they visited us to tell us how happy they were and how they had found the reason to live. We tried to visit them the following week, but the house looked so eerie we became scared and returned home. When we finally combatted our fears and visited them, we found that Janie was absolutely radiant. We had a wonderful time and even joined in the chanting. We returned to evening classes and Sunday feasts often after first getting high. I became interested, and could see that the temple offered a beautiful way of life. We put up pictures of Krsna and the swami in our apartment, offered our food, listened to the records, and read the books. Chuck still forbade me to read certain ones, but he told me nice stories about Krsna. He began to preach to all his friends, even though we were living off big grass deals. (He was finally dealing in kilos.)

One day Janie called me on the phone and asked me to visit her and bring food. I brought her cream cheese and olive sandwiches which she ate as though she was starving. She hated it in the temple, resented being told what to do, and felt they were killing her baby. Janie used to eat candy bars and popcorn against the rules and Bill would beat her. A husband is allowed to beat his wife, since the wife's position is to be subservient to him. She is too low to be subservient to Krsna; only a man can serve God. Bill would run around the temple screaming that she was in maya. This would cause a commotion with the new members, and she would tell people not to join, claiming the devotees were evil and worshipped money. They would not let her leave the temple until her mother came and got her, threatening to call the police. Bill and some devotees went to Janie's home to get her back, but her family called the police. Finally, Janie had the baby and divorced Bill. Bill remained in the temple for a while, but was attached to LSD and tripped in the temple, so they threw him out. He wandered the streets for a while and one day it was learned that he was in a mental hospital.[3] At the time, everybody thought Janie was crazy, especially Chuck. I helped her, but did not believe her.

Finally, Chuck found an eighteen-year-old college student for sex. He sent me to the temple to overcome my grief, and it helped. I wanted to go and live there

---

[3] The researcher ran into Sri Bill, as the devotees liked to call him, on several occasions. One instance was at the Process, another counter-culture church, where he had gone for free food and was looking for a place to sleep for the night.

alone, but could not force myself to leave Chuck. He finally left the girl when he saw I could become a devotee, and we made a concentrated effort—but not total—'cause one day in June he disappeared to join alone. I followed him and overcame him with cries and protestations similar to an Indian epic. Still we did not join together. He had to take one last LSD trip without me, and took two kinds of LSD while visiting the New Hampshire mountains. He chanted because even the woods became ugly to him. The chanting was all that saved him from freaking out completely. I cried, knowing it was over for both of us together. To him it seemed as though I was always crying, but I felt something bad was going to happen to him, and he would not listen to me. I feared the unknown in him, and wondered what new scheme he was planning.

Chuck bought japa beads on which to chant his daily rounds. We both went to chant at the temple and Chuck went out chanting on the street with the devotees, while I would lie in bed at home, exhaused. We both accepted my poor health as normal. One day Chuck had a fight with a bus driver, and by the time we were home he announced that we were joining the temple. I thought that I would be happy, but instead, I cried. I had to give up my home, my cat, my plant; everything! Little did I know I'd lost him, too!

Before we could join the temple together, we had to get married. My mother was the only one who attended the civil ceremony. The next day we moved into the temple. We moved in on a Sunday, feeling joyous and happy. We sold or gave away nearly all of our material possessions. We brought only a few clothes and our books: two *Gitas*, the *Srimad-Bhagavatam, Nectar of Devotion, Journey to Other Planets*, recipes the devotees had given me, prayers and directions on how to mark the body with tilaka. We also brought a Bible and Leary's *The Psychedelic Experience*. At the door I told Chuck that this was an important step and was for life, not something you get into and out of quickly. I also hassled him because he had not given everything up; he still had two hundred dollars in the bank.

The devotees gave us a room together, a bare bleak room in a drafty old building which was once a funeral home. We slept on sleeping bags on the floor

Dishing out the prasada.

with Chuck's grandmother's quilt. We fixed the room up a bit with pictures of Krsna and the swami, and with incense and flowers. We formed sort of a small altar of our own with these things. Then we were separated and shown how to wear the dhoti and sari. We had brought our own material for our garments because as householders we did not expect the temple to provide for us. I hated the sari. Previous to this I had worn only dresses to work, and usually wore blue jeans the rest of the time. How vulnerable one feels in a long wrapped dress, especially when one never quite gets the hang of putting it on properly. I was then transported to the Commons to chant, and "went into ecstasy" when my husband appeared in a dhoti, all shaved up. He was so proud of his shaved head, but I nearly vomited at his new appearance. He really turned my stomach. We chanted, but were quite separate because I was forced into the front line with the other girls. We returned to the temple for the Sunday feast and found that some of our friends had come to visit with us and Bill, who was then still a devotee. We told our friends how happy we were. When they left we felt quite lonely, and really hoped they would join us there.

The next day we rose before the sun was up and went to separate bathrooms to take cold showers. I felt miserable, but this feeling left when the morning chanting of rounds started, and we circumambulated the temple three times in the cold dawn morning. Then there were more rounds and breakfast at 7:00 A.M. As new devotees we were showered with flower garlands. (Bill once said he liked to leave the temple and return because of the attention one received on returning.) After breakfast, from 8:00 A.M. to 9:00 A.M. was temple clean-up time. But on this day I had orders from my husband to find out what happened to his suitcase of clothes. Someone had apparently stolen his pants. The temple president accused Bill, so there was nothing much we could do about it, but it was a shock to discover that the devotees had gone through our suitcase and taken things from it when we were out chanting. The daily routine continued with classes, street chanting, chores, prasada, and so on. The men and women always took prasada separately, but Chuck and I would often displease the devotees by eating together on the front porch.

As time wore on I could not preach or beg for money on the streets anymore. My husband did not force me because he thought preaching was for the men, and he had a secret fear that I would be a better devotee than he. Often I would leave the chanting party to rest alone on the grass and have a few minutes to myself to be with nature and God again. The devotees used to hassle me about this, but my husband allowed it and I was under his authority. I began to stay in the temple a lot, helping the pujari make clothes for Radha and Krsna, shopping, or preparing flowers for the altar. At one point I complained bitterly because I did not see my husband and could not serve him or prepare his food as a proper wife should. So it was decided that I could cook for the whole temple. Chuck did not wish me to do this, saying I was not elevated enough. But the temple president understood my plight and allowed me to help in the kitchen. Even this did not keep me happy for long because I became used to the schedule and grew tired of being told what to do by everyone. Besides, I was still quite agitated because I thought my husband had found a new lover in Krsna, and I told him so. I had preconceived notions about the right way to worship God, and believed it should be of one's free will and not on command. Chuck disagreed with me and was content to take orders, while I would take orders only from him. He was angry, and told me to listen to the women and learn to be a good devotee.

Mornings were presenting a problem for me and I was having a terrible time each day coping with this life. The devotees started taking roll call at morning aratrika and placing guards at the entrance of the temple. I felt like I was in prison. I freaked out once and ran for the door. The president[4] stopped me and I argued my point with him; he agreed and roll call was stopped.

<hr>

[4] The researcher has observed this president to be an extraordinary man, blessed with special understanding and tolerance for others, plus a great talent for managing the prac-

I also used to fall asleep at aratrika and this caused the devotees to clang karatals in my ears. Not too pleasant! I really hated mornings and the cold showers, and I ached so much that I needed aspirins. The devotees told me to take vitamins, and I wondered why I should need them if the food is so pure and perfect. I got very sick and weak, and had no menstrual periods at all. My stomach got big and bloated to the point where I thought I was pregnant. I would go to see a doctor frequently, alone. My husband allowed it, but the devotees did not like it.

Bill eventually stopped following the rules, and did as he pleased. He often sought refuge in our room because only married couples had rooms of their own.[5] All he ever did in my room was write poems and letters to Janie, and read books. But my husband fought with him over this because Bill was supposed to have no contact at all with women.

It had reached the point where all the beauty and pleasure were gone for me, and I was only suffering pain and misery. I could not believe that God wanted us to live like that. One really had to work to get fixed up for the day, whereas before I joined, it was no problem at all. I wanted to move out, but Chuck was happy in the temple, following orders (hard for me to believe, but he was). In the evenings we were usually too tired to talk, and my husband would not allow me to touch him at all. It was very difficult for me to understand the change in him. On some evenings there were householder meetings which I enjoyed. My husband would not go to these; he simply chanted during this time and explained to me that he could not relate to the householders because he was a brahmacari. He never wore the yellow dhoti of the married men. I should have known then! At the householder meetings child care was discussed because there were two pregnant women in the temple and one child. The men devotees thought it would be a lovely idea for the mothers to put their babies in a miniature day care center. One mother would nurse all the babies and do her prescribed duty, and then, the next day, another mother would nurse all the babies and do her prescribed duties. These women had exclusive jobs in ISKCON; one as an expert typist, the other as a cook. I freaked, because Srila Prabhupada's teachings mention nothing of wet nurses, and children are not taken from their mothers until the age of five. Well, one expectant father spoke up (my husband refused to let me speak) and said that he felt that for the first six months the babies should be with the mother and after that he personally would like to watch his own baby. After all, these were special babies elevated enough to take birth in ISKCON.

After the meeting I ran to my room and argued with my husband, who said it did not matter to him since we were not having children. I was so angry at the principle of it all, and how everything was for the good of ISKCON—pure communism—and the men taking over what was clearly a woman's realm! I ran down the stairs in tears to leave the society. One of the expectant mothers stopped and talked to me, and I listened. She said that I should pay no attention to the men; that they didn't know what they were talking about and would soon realize it. Wait and see. Every time I would try to leave, this woman would talk me out of it with the same logic.

For a while I was allowed to care for the one child in the temple on certain days. Pure joy. She was such a lovely and devoted child and had been taught to say Prabhupada and Krsna when she was shown their pictures.

Generally, life was very boring for me, and I would disappear to my room to rest. Finally, the devotees couldn't stand it and put me to work in the afternoons making flower garlands for Radha and Krsna. When I started doing this I met a

---

ticalities of life in the temple. He is considered by everyone to be one of the finest devotees in the movement and has now been elevated by Prabhupada to sannyasi.

[5] This has now been changed by Bhaktivedanta Swami, and couples can no longer together in the temples. A few now rent rooms outside of the temple, but close by. At the communal farm of New Vrndavana, couples may live together as grhasthas.

sixteen-year-old Catholic girl whose name I do not remember. She could not accept gods of the sky and water, and so on. We used to talk karmi talk and discuss our grievances with the way of life we were living. She, too, was ill. We used to read the Bible together, and agreed that the temple's way was the wrong way to worship God. She left before I did.

At the end of August we went to New Vrndavana for the festival of Janmastami. Chuck and I traveled alone on the bus because we had missed the ride with the other devotees. It was our first ride alone together. We talked some and he preached to me, reaffirming that he wanted me with him. I accepted his authority, and by the time we arrived in West Virginia I was happy again. I kissed the ground at New Vrndavana—it was beautiful, and Srila Prabhupada had walked there. I was happy at New Vrndavana in spite of the cold nights. The conditions were primitive, to say the least, but so beautiful out in the country with flowers, fields, mountains, and cows. We had to sleep outside and there were no toilets or showers, so we bathed in a stream. There were four new sannyasas at New Vrndavana and they preached Srila Prabhupada was God himself on the earth, and we should worship him better and follow his orders better. They claimed that Prabhupada had left this country to go to India and Japan and had disappeared from us because we were not good devotees. The older devotees would not allow these sannyasis to preach such blasphemy and stopped the meetings. All the temple presidents got together, held long private meetings, and the next day a telegram was received from Prabhupada saying he had not left the society, but had gone away to write, do his work as a swami, and preach all over the world. He left matters in the hands of a governing board, the GBC. The four sannyasis were asked to change their preaching that Prabhupada was God. The devotees argued that this was the last trap of maya. Maya tries to convince you that all is one, but the devotees are personalists and believe in separate and personal identities for their souls, and most certainly for God's. Of course, this is one big contradiction to their way of life in the temple, but they don't see it as such.

It was all very confusing and questions began to pop into my mind. The devotees often would discuss Srila Prabhupada's bodily disappearance and his relation to Krsna, so I began to wonder if he would rise as Christ rose on His death. Who was Srila Prabhupada in relation to Christ? I got my answers at New Vrndavana, at least I thought so. If Srila Prabhupada was God, then I should surrender and follow because he was Christ reincarnated. Now, if the sannyasis were wrong, who was Srila Prabhupada and why should I surrender to him?

We fasted for the twenty-four hours on Janmastami with only lemon juice to wet our throats. We spent all day chanting in the temple, offering obeisances, prayers, and poems of gratitude to the swami for saving us from material death. Everyone was a little confused by the disagreements that had arisen and the fact that Srila Prabhupada did not attend, but things picked up at the wedding ceremonies and the big feast that ended the holiday. It was over. I did not want to leave, but my husband said that the weather was too bad to stay there, and we returned to the city with the devotees.

I was happy for a few more weeks, but could not get the talks out of my mind no matter how much the devotees would explain and explain to me. I wanted to disappear, take another acid trip, so that then I could be subservient, but I didn't. Then one day in late September, while chanting on the Cambridge Common, I could not stop watching the hippies who were busy with music, sex, and getting high. I felt lonely for the old way of life and decided to walk back to my old apartment and talk to my friends, and maybe take LSD. But just then, my husband saw me wandering around. I ran into the church across the street and called my parents. I asked my mother to send someone to visit me or to write to me. I was surprised when my mother appeared that night at the feast. She asked Chuck if I could take a walk with her, and when we got outside my father was parked there in his car. I shouldn't have been surprised because he would never allow my mother to drive to the city. He told me that he had had a bad dream that I was dying and needed his help. They drove me home. I was still wearing a purple sari and my bead bag. I went because I was too weak to fight. Actually, I had no idea what was going on, or that I had left my husband and the temple. When we got home my father threw my things in the trash, fed me a meatless meal, and put me to bed.

The next day, when we went shopping, I was so weak that my parents took me to see a doctor. I passed out during a blood test, and went home to bed to read my Bible, talk to Christ, and die in peace. I prayed to Jesus, and just as He was coming to take my soul away, my parents rushed me to the hospital, where I spent five days sleeping, only being awakened for food and a blood pressure reading. What a drag. I could not even die in peace! They fed me intravenously because I was near starvation.

When I returned to my parents' home from the hospital, Chuck appeared to take me back to the temple. I had to tell him that I had now accepted Christ and did not believe in the swami anymore. There was a fight between my father and Chuck. My father called the police to prevent himself from killing Chuck. I had to choose between my husband and my family, so I chose my husband and left. I had a job to do; to save Chuck. I now believed that Christ had saved me and that it was His will that I save my husband. Christ would give me the power to save Chuck from the fires of eternal damnation because he had not accepted Jesus, but had accepted a false prophet as his savior.

I refused to go back to the temple and he took me to the house of some friends where we had a wild fight. He dragged me down a flight of stairs when I called the deities idols and committed all sorts of blasphemy. The friends called the temple, and Chuck was told to return to the temple, which he did. Then our friends and I had a talk. I told them all my problems and was glad I did because the husband was ready to leave his wife and new baby to join the temple.

The next day Chuck returned. We spent the night together and talked, but to no avail. He told me to leave him in the morning, and that it would be "forever." Of course it was not forever, but then again it was, because we never got back together. Instead, for two long years we quarreled violently over his being a devotee and my change in religion. Chuck gave me sixty dollars and I rented a room in a friend's apartment near the temple.

Then Chuck's mother visited from overseas. Before she left she told me to leave him alone because he was happy, and to start a new life of my own, but I could not. I was so heartbroken. When she left I went back to my old job, and continued to visit Chuck at the temple. We would often quarrel violently, like the time I learned that while I was in the hospital, Chuck had been tried and acquitted on draft evasion charges. For a minute I was happy and believed he'd leave ISKCON, but I saw that he really liked being in the orange religious military order of Krsna and the swami. I was shocked because he had claimed he could never follow orders, otherwise he'd be in the service. During this time I would always cry and carry on and freak 'cause I was married to him, he was my husband, and it was forever. The only way I could possibly save him was to show him, by example, that the material way of life was not killing me, and that Krsna did not kill me for leaving the temple. Then one day I freaked out badly. He was preaching about Krsna, and I started to carry on about the Bible preaching to the other people and discrediting his words. He told me to go and I refused and screamed, "Fuck the deities, fuck Srila Prabhupada, and fuck Krsna." It almost got me killed. The devotees had to drag me out of the temple, but I clung to the door screaming. Finally, my husband slugged me and threw me off the porch. Then he jumped down, dragged me off the temple property to the parking lot next door, and tried to make me stand up so he could fight me like a man. But I refused to stand, and just as he started in to beat me for real, the temple president grabbed him, threw him inside the temple, and locked me out. That was it! The president said I would not be allowed to return to the temple again. I stood on the street crying bitter lonely tears. After a while, one male devotee emerged and talked to me until I calmed down. This boy had always been kind to me, but my husband never liked him and they used to fight frequently. Finally, exhausted, I left. When I tried to return, I was not allowed back and my husband was shipped away without a word of where he was. After months he called me and said that all was forgiven, but up until then I was frantic.

At this point Chuck was initiated as Janardana, and I began to see a change in his behavior as a devotee. Now he seemed more committed than ever. The swami asked for devotees who could raise the money to go to India, and Janardana was somehow, I don't know how, able to raise the money. He visited all the places sacred to Lord Krsna, swam in the Ganges, and was only one hundred miles from the Himalayas. Janardana received his second initiation in India. He became a brahmin and was given the gayatri mantra, a mantra which is all his own and which he chants three times a day in silence, holding onto his brahmana thread in a special manner. He was thrilled to have received this initiation at the auspicious time of the full moon, and in India by his spiritual master. But he was so nervous about being in his spiritual master's pure radiant light and presence that he made a mistake during the ceremony. The kindly swami laughed and said, "Let it go. He will catch on in time." I could see that Janardana had changed in India and that he was not as proud now as he was when he first became a devotee with me. He changed on this night of his second initiation, becoming more in tune with himself and the world around him. He now realized himself as only a poor servant in relation to the greatness of his spiritual master. He became more confident of himself as a devotee, and in his relations with other devotees. He learned to accept his wife's need to remain in maya in the material world. He became calmer and more accepting of things in general, unless they were a threat to his own consciousness. He, at last, was becoming pure, and treating people as he himself wished to be treated (something he had never learned to do before). He learned another lesson as a result of serious illness contracted in India. He suffered jaundice and dysentery, and these afflictions made him realize how essential it is to care for his body. Previous to this he did not believe in caring for the body, and he now suffered disagreements with fellow devotees, who still had not come to realize this. He lay in a sick-bed set off from the others, alone under mosquito netting for a long time. All he could do was chant. He was almost at the point of death before he received medical attention and proper care.

As he grew better he began to go into the market alone to buy his food (which he cooked himself), for a special diet designed to aid his recovery. Janardana wrote to me to send some money for his food as the temple could not provide the special food he needed. He loved to cook and tried to learn all he could about cooking the delicious foodstuffs offered to the deities in India. He loved India in spite of the unclean temples and the professional pujaris with their materialistic ways and big bellies, and their arrogant attitude toward this "American fake brahmin." Janardana saw that the people in the cities were becoming more westernized and hateful of these devotees who were trying to turn people back to the old religion. One day he was stoned by some villagers on his way to the public toilets, but he managed to escape without injury. Another day in the urinal he met a brahmin who attempted to give him a beating. It was not pleasant in the city. The violence was heavy there and often sankirtana parties turned to street fights. There was one such fight in which the Indians stormed the temple, and the devotees had to defend themselves. But the swami was Indian, and he went out and talked to his people, and there was no more violence. Even the monkeys were against the American devotees. They would steal the devotees' beadbags, and one had to bribe them with food to get the beads back. Clubs were kept in the temple to hit the monkeys with and chase them out.

Even with all this, for Janardana it was beautiful in the country. Usually the people came to watch the devotees, and to chant, dance, and listen to Prabhupada and learn from him. The old people were the most elevated. There was one group of shaven-headed women who lived on the riverbank in Vrndavana and chanted and begged and slept on the ground where Lord Krsna walked. They were old and sick, yet out of love for Krsna they lived like this.

The temple life in India is more relaxed and not as strict as it is in the States. The business of the temple is to solicit life members, attend lectures and parties, speak in public, and bring the deities into people's homes. But life there is very hard for an American devotee, confronted as he is with hostility, poverty, and sickness. One has no recourse but to chant and think of the guru and Krsna constantly. Often, though, the devotees quarrel over petty things when their attention wavers from thoughts of Krsna. Luckily, Janardana managed to remain totally Krsna-conscious and totally integrated in his own personality, even as he was becoming aware of what the temple was really like with their orders and lack of compassion for fellow members. He became aware, also, that the government of India and most of the educated people were against this religion because they want industrialization and food, and the two do not seem to go together.

It is confusing to be in India where there are so many spiritual masters, each claiming to be perfect. Janardana did not wander off in search of adventure, or to learn from other spiritual masters, as some devotees are prone to do. Many devotees quickly return to the USA because they do not like the country. Others bloop in India. But for Janardana it was a true religious pilgrimage, and he left when his visa expired in hopes of being allowed to return again.

Soon after Janardana's return, I was informed that the FBI was looking for him again on new charges. This time it was for his failure to report his change of address for three months during 1967. Janardana turned himself in and was released on personal recognizance until his November trial. Ten days before his twenty-sixth birthday, he was brought to trial and sent to a mental hospital. He went away calmly, without a word or a look at me. I went into a total mental depression and went on welfare, since I could no longer work. All I did was hibernate in my rented room for the entire winter. By the time Janardana wrote to me in January, I had decided to divorce him. All the letters I received from him while in the hospital were about Krsna, and from their tone I could tell that he only wanted to see the devotees, not me. He mainly wrote me for money to buy peanuts, since he still was not eating meat. In May I received a letter from him asking me to visit him and bring fifty dollars. By then he was not eating anything except cereal and was so weak he could hardly stand. For him, the stay in the hospital was another test of his faith, and provided a great opportunity to preach to the other patients.

I was afraid that Janardana might die, so I took the trip to the hospital, only to have to wait for hours because they could not find my husband. Of course they thought at first that he was just out in the woods, chanting somewhere. I was sure that he was dead in the woods, and I was having a hard time sitting there without going out to look for him myself. After they searched and could not find him, he was declared an escaped prisoner and dangerous. That weekend there were heavy rains in the region, so I was doubly worried. Besides, they just did not care about him. No one knew if he ate, or what he ate. So he disappeared, and I grieved for a half a year as a proper widow. If he is dead, he is with Krsna in the spiritual sky. I no longer believe that he is damned in hell 'cause he had refused Christ because, in time, he accepted Christ as a prophet, and he himself had totally changed into a great and good devotee. If he did escape, he did it to preserve his Krsna Consciousness. So I've let him go, and plan to start a new life for myself in California, and maybe someday remarry. Of course, I cannot sue the government for his death because I have no proof. Either way, I am sure he is with Krsna.

Note: Yvonne returned to the movement two years after she left and was later initiated.

Conclusions

I offer my humble obeisances unto His Divine Grace Prabhupada A. C. Bhaktivedanta Swami . . .
who defied cheap popular adoration by truthfully telling the youth of America
that to have Krsna the soul must be pure, free of everything,
who with his disciples untiringly worships Sri, Sri Radha and Krsna in their
temple. (Hayagriva dasa Adhikari)

We have systematically examined the culture of ISKCON and the life
histories of some individuals who have joined an ISKCON temple. A dominating
motif running through these life histories appears to be disenchantment with
society at large. Loss of individuality, loss of interest in making money, and feelings
of isolation cause these individuals to place themselves in the well-defined structural and ideological setting of an ISKCON temple where they can realize a more
meaningful identity. Do a person's experiences within ISKCON enhance one's
psychosocial development or retard it? The biographical data illustrates that an
individual's personal history prior to entrance into ISKCON will pattern his success or failure as a devotee. All devotees, potential devotees, and blooped devotees
want to change both themselves and their social milieu. Some individuals, such
as Diane, are severely limited by their earlier experiences and relationships and
are beyond the type of personal rehabilitation offered by ISKCON. They are unable
to make a satisfactory adjustment, either within ISKCON or outside of it.

Successful devotees may or may not remain devotees forever; but for the first
time in their lives they have experienced a coherent identity and status within
ISKCON. Although the life experiences within ISKCON are very different from
those in the rest of society, positive growth experiences within ISKCON will carry
over, affecting the individual's reentry into society at large. Those who remain in
ISKCON have attained sufficient satisfaction and happiness to keep them there.
Even if one leaves the temple, he may nevertheless have been successful in redefining his identity and leaves as a stronger personality.

Bhaktivedanta's teachings are novel enough to catch the interest of a large seg-
ment of disenchanted youth. Before they come under the swami's influence, these
young people have already developed a sophisticated interest in nonwestern culture
from their education, reading, and foreign travel. Many of them have traveled to
India, sought other philosophies, tried to alter their consciousness with drugs, and
practiced other forms of yoga and vegetarianism before they are drawn to Vedic
culture.

Bhaktivedanta, with the help of his disciples, has successfully transplanted Vedic culture in America with as few errors in transmission as possible. He has made only the most necessary compromises in order to render this essentially Hindu system operable in the West. The swami has, on many occasions, vetoed the suggestions of his followers and has continually emphasized the importance of the Vedic acarya system which ideally hands down the teachings and scripture from one guru to the next completely unchanged.

Naturally, ISKCON has found that some compromises are unavoidable, and one example of this is begging practices. Begging is a traditional function of a Hindu monk, and in India this practice is supported by a social system which educates people to be aware of their duty to give rice, food, or money to the mendicants. The American devotees of Krsna have quickly learned that begging in the United States is difficult or impossible because people become angry and refuse to give; moreover, in many places it is against the law. The practice of begging has not been dropped entirely, but the financial success of the incense business has necessarily replaced it as the economic mainstay of the organization.

Most of ISKCON's compromises have been economic. Within the individual asramas, fewer compromises are made. Here every effort is made to follow the rituals down to the smallest details. Thus, visitors to the temple are exposed to unadulterated Indian ritual in which no attempt is made to dilute the ceremonies for visitors. The devotees will patiently explain anything about which a visitor might be curious, but they will also pressure him to participate in chanting, dancing, taking prasadam, and attending scripture classes. They will urge him to participate in Tulasi Devi worship and in the swing ceremony (Jhulana-yatra) no matter how ridiculous the visitor may think these rites to be. It is the exotic practices that have, after all, drawn many of the devotees to the temple in the first place.

Some Indian visitors to the ISKCON services have remarked that the American devotees follow ritual more closely than do their Indian counterparts. These visitors, however, object to the devotees' insistence on silence in the temple during ceremonials. They say that in India they can talk in the temple if they are so inclined. One Indian woman observed that Indian devotees are more respectful and humble in their bhevaior. "But," she said, "these American devotees are listening nice and behaving nice, so they are better than the rest of the American kids." Parochialism is maintained in the more important features such as ceremonies, while small details may be changed according to need. Many of the ceremonial items are ordered from India if there is no equivalent item made in the U.S. or if the item is better made in India. The deity figurines are ordered from India, as are the camara and much of the incense used in aratrika. Clothes from India are worn whenever possible. All food (prasada) is cooked according to Indian vegetarian recipes, although in times of emergency, compromises are made. When the stove in one asrama broke down, the devotees ate salads and uncooked foods in contrast to the usual complex preparations. Some American foods have been declared by the guru to be Vedic, such as popcorn. The popcorn edict was received with great joy by the devotees.

The institution of marriage, which is basic to Vedic culture, has fared badly in American asramas, and married couples no longer cohabitate in the temples except under the special circumstances which are outlined in the chapter on marriage.

Devotees can now marry or not as they please, and there seems to be a direct trend away from marriage among the devotees.

An important theme underlying all of the life histories presented in this text is the theme of satiation and revulsion with sense gratification and the permissive values of our society. Krsna Consciousness not only offers an organized framework for developing a new life style counter to the dominant culture but, in addition, offers a complete alternative to the youth subculture. Krsna Consciousness, as one young observer expressed it, "is counter-counter-culture." Another youthful visitor to the temple noted, "They (the Hare Krsnas) are out to freak-out the freaks (hippies)!" We quickly learn from the ISKCON members that they have played out drugs and sex at an early age and now want to change these aspects of their lives completely. They are demanding less rather than more freedom. A child psychoanalyst, Ira Mintz (1973: 64), has cited the popularity of the Hare Krsna movement as an escape from permissive sexual mores and notes: "Under the guise of a religious commitment [we have] a strict, ascetic society with a built-in set of controls." ISKCON with its high degree of institutionalization and puritanism is an effective refuge from the confusion of today's society. This theory is well supported by the life history material given in this study.

THE FUTURE OF ISKCON

Inevitably, the question is asked: what is the future of ISKCON?

The seed Bhaktivedanta has planted has taken root within the fertile soil of America's dissatisfied youth and is growing rapidly. One can only guess what future direction ISKCON will take. Not even Bhaktivedanta himself knows with certainty what will happen after his death. We know that the spiritual master has taken definite steps to insure the continuation of the movement, and that the GBC is well prepared to act on the old guru's instructions in the event of his death. What these steps are and who will succeed Bhaktivedanta are closely guarded secrets which may be revealed to the GBC only after the guru dies. The devotees avoid discussing the subject, and few of them indulge in speculation concerning the future. All they feel free to say is that a spiritual master will appear automatically by his own power when he is needed. It is safe to assume that Bhaktivedanta remembers his experiences with the Gaudiya Vaisnava Maths, when someone other than himself was recognized as the acarya after Saraswati's death.[1] Bhaktivedanta also recalls the ensuing violent arguments and the court battles[2] which followed them. Saraswati has also established a governing board similar to the GBC, but had failed to designate his successor. It is not unusual, however, for an Indian guru to appoint a successor if he thinks his end is near. It is said that "one lamp lights another," so the new acarya is usually the old guru's closest disciple, and I think that Bhaktivedanta will choose someone like Vasudeva to follow him.

If the GBC agrees with Bhaktivedanta's choice, things may proceed smoothly, and the new guru will take over the Society and continue as he was instructed to

[1] See chapter 2, p. 15.
[2] It is common for a dispute involving guru succession to be brought into an Indian court of law for settlement.

do. If there is a disagreement among the GBC, or even if the ordinary devotees cannot accept the new guru, there might be a factional split which could lead to the demise of ISKCON. There is also the possibility that the GBC will try to legitimize Bhaktivedanta's choice by claiming that Bhaktivedanta was an avatara or an incarnation of Krsna. The devotees presently recognize Srila Prabhupada's ambiguous status and say such things as, "A bona fide spiritual master is not an ordinary person. If a disciple does not understand the transcendental nature of his spiritual master, then it is better for him not to accept a spiritual master." In this way there is an opening for Bhaktivedanta, after death, to be proclaimed an avatara.

Proclaiming Bhaktivedanta an avatara will create new problems because the *Srimad-Bhagavatam* is specific about the appearance of the next major incarnation. "Thereafter, at the conjunction of the two yugas, the Lord of the creation will take His birth as Kalki incarnation becoming the son of Vishnu Joshi, when the rulers of the earth shall convert into almost to the rank of the plunderers" (Bhaktivedanta 1972a: First Canto, Ch. 3, 164).

Kalki, Bhaktivedanta says informally to his devotees, will be the last incarnation of Krsna and will appear at the end of this age of Kali-yuga. The end of Kali-yuga[3] will be 427,000 years from the present, and by then the human species will have fallen so low that people will be killing and eating their own children;[4] they will have shrunk to a height of two feet; they will have a life span of twenty years; and none of these men will have the mental ability to understand philosophy or scriptures. The only salvation for this fallen race is to be killed directly by God. Kalki will appear on a white horse and slay all the fallen souls who will be automatically liberated, and will ascend directly to the spiritual sky. The devotees will have been living in underground caves during this terrible age to escape the fallen generation who would kill them on sight. The devotees will be especially dear to Krsna because they did not wait for the final stage of Kali-yuga to become God-conscious.

Bhaktivedanta is very free in his interpretation of scripture. This we can see from the above Kalki passage, elaborated from a simple statement which tells only when the incarnation will appear, who his father will be, and that men will be reduced to plunderers. The devotees not only willingly accept such a story, but cherish it as special privileged information given to them by their beloved guru.

If these spiritual passages are open to such liberal interpretations, then we can expect no difficulty in freely interpreting scripture to "prove" that Bhaktivedanta is an avatara. Such interpretation would introduce nothing new, but would serve to clarify the poorly understood ambiguity about the nature of the spiritual master. The following passage from the *Srimad-Bhagavatam* makes such an interpretation possible: "Oh Brahmins, the incarnations of the Lord are innumerable as much as there are innumerable rivulets coming out of the inexhaustable sources of water" (Bhaktivedanta 1972b: 187). Bhaktivedanta (1972a: 164) in his purport to the above passage, clears the path for another incarnation:

---

[3] The duration of Kali-yuga is 432,000 years and 5,000 years have passed, leaving a remaining 427,000 years.

[4] A devotee remarked that eating children is not so far fetched because people are already eating their mothers and fathers, the cow and the bull. The other animals eaten are our brothers and sisters who were born with a lower intelligence due to bad karma in their past lives; therefore, meat eating today is just a step away from eating our children.

The incarnations of the personality of Godhead as they are mentioned herein before are not complete list. (*sic*)

The Lord is an inexhaustible source for innumerable incarnations which are not always mentioned but such incarnations are distinguished by specific extraordinary performances which are impossible to be done by any living being.

Worsley (1968: xiv) explains that a prophet can die, be imprisoned, or resign his role as leader, and a movement can continue without his guidance. From this, Partridge (1973: 81) concludes, "Traits of personal charisma, skills of leadership, or force of personality are apparently not the critical ingredients.[5] What is needed, perhaps, are conditions of deprivation and hardship, a doctrine or message formulated out of cultural traditions, and a ritual for reducing high levels of stress and reinforcing belief in the doctrine." Research such as the above indicates that some social movements will continue without leadership. But in the case of ISKCON this would not be possible, since a spiritual master is an absolutely essential ingredient of the Vedic system that Bhaktivedanta presents. In order to gain perfect knowledge one has to approach the proper person, and this person is a guru.

The life style, ideology, and ritual of ISKCON should continue to appeal to youth so long as they remain liminal people in modern society, so long as the lack of value orientation and stresses of modern society persist. The entire guru explosion, the "Jesus freaks," Zen, and other cults will also continue to appeal to youth while conditions in modern society remain intolerable to large numbers of people. It seems certain that these "new" religions have only just begun, and it is impossible for us to evaluate the strength they are gaining. It is also difficult to determine how they will influence our society, although it is certain to happen. The new religions teach that a better quality of everyday life is necessary for spiritual advancement, giving youth a reason to choose self-improvement over the emptiness they have found in establishment religions.

[5] When asked what accounts for his popularity and ISKCON's popularity in America, Bhaktivedanta answered, "It is not due to my personality. It is because I am presenting the truth as it is." From an interview written up in "The Search for the Divine" in *Back to Godhead*, No. 49, p. 5.

Appendix I*

Paramparā is the chain of disciplic succession leading to the present ācārya of Kṛṣṇa Consciousness and founder of ISKCON, A. C. Bhaktivedanta Swami.

Kṛṣṇa	Vyāsatītha
Brahmā	Lakṣmīpati
Nārada	Mādhavendra Purī
Vyāsa	Īśvara Purī
Madhva	(Nityānanda, Advaita)**
Padmanābha	*Lord Caitanya*
Nṛhari	Rūpa (Svarūpa, Sanātana)
Mādhava	Raghunātha, Jīva
Akṣobhya	Kṛṣṇadāsa
Jayatīrtha	Narottama
Jñānasindhu	Viśvanātha
Dayānidhi	(Baladeva) Jagannātha
Vidyāndidhi	Bhaktivinode
Rājendra	Guarakiśora
Jayadharma	Bhaktisiddhānta Sarasvatī
Puruṣottama	A. C. Bhaktivedanta Swami
Brahmaṇyatīrtha	

* Diacritical marks are inserted here and in the glossary to indicate pronunciation and a more authentic relation to Sanskrit.

** The devotees say that Nityānanda was an incarnation of Balirama, who they believe is an expansion of Krsna and that Advaita was Nityānanda's devotee. Both appeared with Lord Caitanya as part of his divine incarnation and his expansions. An incarnation is the physical appearance of God in any form at another time. An expansion is God simultaneously taking on as many forms as he wishes. A devotee is a follower.

Appendix II

The works of A. C. Bhaktivendanta Swami:

Bhagavad-gita As It Is 1972

Srimad-Bhagavatam 1972–1975   Cantos 1–4 published in 13 volumes. Canto 5 in preparation.

Sri Caitanya-caritamrta 1973   Adi-lila published in 3 volumes. Madhya-lila and Antya-lila in preparation.

Teachings of Lord Caitanya 1968

Sri Isopanisad 1969

The Nectar of Devotion 1970

Krsna, the Supreme Personality of Godhead (3 volumes) 1970

Easy Journey to Other Planets 1970

Krsna Consciousness: The Topmost Yoga System 1970

The Krsna Consciousness Movement is the Genuine Vedic Way: Correspondence with Dr. J. F. Staal 1970

Transcendental Teachings of Prahlad Maharaja 1972

The Perfection of Yoga 1972

Krsna, the Reservoir of Pleasure 1972

Beyond Birth and Death 1972

On the Way to Krsna 1973

Raja-vidya: The King of Knowledge 1973

Elevation to Krsna Consciousness 1973

Krsna Consciousness: The Matchless Gift 1974

Founder of *Back to Godhead* magazine

All are published by ISKCON Press, 32 Tiffany Place, Brooklyn, N.Y. 11231. The Press was formerly in Boston.

Appendix III

Temple Schedule—New York, N.Y.

A.M.

5:00	Mangala-aratrika
5:30	Japa Mala
6:00	*Srimad-Bhagavatam* class
6:30	*Nectar of Devotion* class
6:45	Prayers to the spiritual master and a taped lecture by Srila Prabhupada
7:15	Japa Mala
8:15	Offering prasada
8:30	Dhoop aratrika
8:45	Devotees take prasada
9:15	Clean-up time
10:30	Sankirtan leaves

P.M.

12:00	Offering prasada
12:15	Bnog aratrika
12:30	Devotees take prasada
4:00	Offering prasada
4:15	Dhoop aratrika
5:30	Devotees take prasada
6:15	*Bhagavad-gita* class
7:00	Sunda aratrika
7:45	Press sankirtan leaves
9:00	Offer prasada
9:15	Aratrika
9:55	Press sankirtan returns

Appendix IV

Locations of ISKCON centers around the world (1975)

AFRICA: Johannesburg, S. Africa; Lusaka, Zambia; Mombassa, Kenya; Nairobi, Kenya; Port Louis, Mauritius

ASIA: Bombay, India; Calcutta, India; Hyderabad, India; Jakarta, Indonesia; Kowloon, Hong Kong; Mayapur, India; New Delhi, India; Taipei, Taiwan; Tehran, Iran; Tokyo, Japan; Vrndavana, India

AUSTRALIA: Adelaide, Aust.; Auckland, New Zealand; Lautoka, Fiji; Melbourne, Aust.; Sydney, Aust.

EUROPE: Amsterdam, Holland; Copenhagen, Denmark; Edinburgh, Scotland; Frankfurt A. Main, W. Germany; Geneva, Switzerland; London, England; Manchester, England; Paris, France; Rome, Italy; Stockholm, Sweden

LATIN AMERICA: Buenos Aires, Argentina; Caracas, Venezuela; Mexico City, Mexico; Rio Piedras, Puerto Rico; Santo Domingo, Dominican Republic; St. Joseph, Trinidad and Tobago

NORTH AMERICA: Ann Arbor, Michigan; Atlanta, Georgia; Austin, Texas; Baltimore, Maryland; Boston, Massachusetts; Boulder Creek, California; Bridesville, British Columbia; Buffalo, New York; Carriere, Mississippi; Chicago, Illinois; Cleveland, Ohio; Dallas, Texas; Denver, Colorado; Detroit, Michigan; Gainesville, Florida; Honolulu, Hawaii; Houston, Texas; Laguna Beach, California; Los Angeles, California; Miami, Florida; Montreal, Quebec; New Orleans, Louisiana; New Vrndavana, W. Virginia; New York, New York; Ottawa, Ontario; Philadelphia, Pennsylvania; Pittsburgh, Pennsylvania; Phoenix, Arizona; Portland, Oregon; Quebec City, Quebec; St. Louis, Missouri; San Diego, California; San Francisco, California; Seattle, Washington; Toronto, Ontario; Vancouver, British Columbia; Washington, D.C.; Winnipeg, Manitoba

As a measure of the movement's growth, the number of centers has increased from thirty-one in 1970, to sixty-three in 1972, to seventy-five in 1975.

Appendix V

Financial Statement of the Boston Temple—March 1972*

Monthly average of incoming and outgoing expenses:

Incoming		Outgoing		
Incense	$ 600.00	Temple maintenance		$ 100.00
Contributions	$ 100.00	Utilities		
Distribution of maga-		(Oil:	$325.00	
zine	$ 600.00	Gas:	$ 75.00	
TOTAL INCOME	$1,300.00	Elec:	$250.00)	$ 650.00
		Truck maintenance and		
		gasoline		$ 150.00
		Prasadam (food)		$ 350.00
		Monthly mortgage		$1,000.00
		Medical expenses		$ 50.00
				$2,300.00

Coming Expenses:

Truck insurance: $300; due to our being late with payment of March mortgage, the owner has demanded an extra payment to be held as permanent security, and this is due April 8th or he will instigate foreclosure for our over-late payment which was made March 16th. This security payment is $1,000. Our devotees are also looking for full-time employment, although the majority are needed to continue operating our Krishna Consciousness missionary work, which is full-time. These figures show that we are operating at a deficit of $1,000 a month. This deficit has only occurred recently. The reason is previously our income from magazine distribution was much higher; we ascribe the low distribution to the economic recession and also people are more and more turning away from religion.

In order to remain in operation we require immediate donations to meet the April 8th deadline for payment of the $1,000 security payment, and we also need regular pledged contributions from sympathetic persons, on a regular basis monthly. Krishna Consciousness Society is producing young men and women of sublime character, who do not take intoxicants of any sort and who do not indulge in illicit sexual activities. Moreover, the center is open for everyone and is offering the top-

* It was printed by ISKCON to help raise money and is now out-of-date.

most welfare activity, taking persons out of material miseries and into the bliss of spiritual life. We are educating, from authoritative sources, how to love God, and that is the ultimate purpose of the human form of life.

HARE KRISHNA HARE KRISHNA KRISHNA KRISHNA HARE HARE
HARE RAMA HARE RAMA RAMA RAMA HARE HARE

Glossary

ācārya: teacher by example

adhikārī: householder

ānanda: absolute bliss

ārātrika: greeting the Lord

arca-vigraha: deity incarnation

āśrama: spiritual community based on Vedic principles

avatāra: incarnation of God

bhāgavata: devotee of Bhagavān Kṛṣṇa

Bhagavad-gītā: "song of God," the sacred book of the Vedic tradition originally comprising the 25th to 42nd chapters of the section on Bhimsa in the *Mahābhārata*. The *Gita* is a synthesis of several strains including the three yogas: jñāna, karma, and bhakti. Many different interpretations are offered which differ slightly, but generally agree that its message involves the ideal of selfless action, true knowledge of reality, and devotion to the Lord.

Bhagavān: God

bhakta: practitioner of bhakti-yoga or devotee

bhakti: fervent devotion to God, a religious discipline or yoga for worshipping a personal God.

bloop: dropping out of ISKCON

Brahmā: the deity who, according to the *Bhagavad-gītā* and *Śrīmad-Bhāgavatam*, is entrusted by Kṛṣṇa with the task of creating the universe. Along with Viṣṇu and Śiva, he is one of the three deities who preside over the creation.

brāhma-muhūrta: one hour and thirty-six minutes before sunrise. This is the most auspicious hour of the day for spiritual advancement.

brahmacārī: a celibate male devotee

brāhmaṇa: priest, priestly caste

cāmara: a yak tail used in ārātrika ceremonies

capatis: a thin pancake-shaped bread made of whole wheat flour and water and roasted on a griddle. This and dahl are staple foods of the Indian diet.

choti: sandalwood paste mark worn on forehead

dahl: a thick soup mixture of lentils and spices

dāsa: male servant

dāsī: female servant

devotee: a member of an ISKCON temple

dharma: duty; the full range of social, moral, and religious obligations in the Vedic tradition

dhoti: draped garment worn by men in place of trousers

ekādaśī: fast day

freaks: a popular name for hippies or any long-haired youths

gāyatrī mantra: the secret mantra that is revealed to a devotee in his brahmin thread ceremony. It is inauspicious to utter it aloud.

GBC: governing board commission of ISKCON

ghee: clarified butter
Godhead: essential and divine nature of God
gopī: cowherd girl
gṛhastha: a householder or married man
guru: spiritual master, teacher
haribol: chant the holy name of Kṛṣṇa
harer-nāma: holy name
ISKCON: The abbreviated form of the title International Society for Kṛṣṇa Con-
    sciousness
iṣṭa–goṣṭi: meeting
jaya: spiritual victory
japa beads: beads for chanting, carried in a small cloth bead bag over the shoulder.
    There are 108 on each string.
jñāna: knowledge
kali-yuga: dark age, the present span of history
karatāls: finger cymbals
karma: the law of morality such that all action inexorably bears a credit or debit
    value on the scale of existence; also referring to the discipline or yoga by
    which individuals can progress spiritually according to the ideal of selfless
    actions
karmī: a person who is not a devotee of ISKCON
kīrtana: Chanting or glorification, including (1) saṅkīrtana—chanting aloud, or
    (2) chanting softly and slowly with japa beads
Kṛṣṇa: the deity regarded by the Hare Kṛṣṇa movement as the Supreme Person-
    ality of Godhead. Popularly revered throughout India, he is the speaker of
    Bhagavad-gītā and Śrīmad-Bhāgavatam.
Kṛṣṇa–loka: residence of Kṛṣṇa
kunti-mala: small tulasi wood beads worn around the neck
laksmī: the goddess of fortune; a term also used for money
līlās: pastimes of the Deity
mahā: great
Mahābhārata: one of the two great epics of India (the other is the *Ramayana*); a
    compilation of history, folklore, ethics, and some philosophical sections, one of
    which constitutes the *Bhagavad-gītā*
mahārāja: title used for sannyāsa in ISKCON, literally great king
mahātmā: great soul
mangala-ārātrika: the early-morning ārātrika, the first of the day
mantra: a sacred formula, chant, or incantation addressed to a deity
maṭha: temple
māyā: illusion, phenomenal world
mṛdanga: drum used in sankīrtana
mukti: liberation
paramparā: disciplic succession
prabhu: master, used as a term of address by the devotees for one another
prabhupāda: one at whose feet many masters sit
prasāda: remnants of food offerings to the Deities; also called mercy by the
    devotees
prema: love
pujārī: caretaker of the Deities, must be a brahmin
rasa: one's eternal relationship with Kṛṣṇa
sādhu: holy man of spotless character
samādhi: absorption in God Consciousness
saṁsāra: transmigration of souls; also called the wheel
sankīrtana: *see* kirtana
sannyāsa: renounced order of spiritual life
sannyāsī: a renounced person; same as swami

sari: long draped garment worn by women fashioned from a six-yard length of cloth

śāstra: scripture

śikha: lock of hair left on the otherwise shaved head of a male devotee

Śiva: *see* Brahmā; god of destruction of all cosmic processes and rhythms

Śrī: a title of reverence

Śrīmatī: female form of Śrī

svāhā: a syllable similar in usage to amen

swāmī: one who controls his senses; *see* sannyāsā

tapasya: penance, austerity

tilaka: clay resembling fuller's earth used to mark the body

Upaniṣad: a collection of philosophical texts, believed to number between one and two hundred

vaikuṇṭha: the spiritual planets

vānaprastha: retired order; retired from family life

vedānta: end point of the *Vedas*; the system of philosophy based on the *Upaniṣads*

Vedas: knowledge derived from the Vedic hymns, including the *Upaniṣads*, which form the basis of most Hindu philosophical and religious systems

Viṣṇu: *see* Brahmā; conceived primarily as the pervader or sustainer of the universe

vyāsāsana: the spiritual master's chair

yoga: a physical, mental, and spiritual discipline leading to the union of the individual mind with the supreme or cosmic consciousness

yuga: age; *see* kali-yuga

Note: These spellings are preferred by the members of ISKCON. Being translations from Sanskrit, they are not the only spellings.

References

Aberle, David F., 1966, *The Peyote Religion among the Navaho*. Viking Fund Publications in Anthropology, No. 42. New York: Wenner-Gren Foundation.

Adhikari, Hayagriva dasa, "Chant," Part 1, *Back to Godhead*, No. 36, pp. 24–26.

Barnett, G., 1957, *Indian Shakers and Messianic Cults of the Pacific Northwest*. Carbondale, Ill.: Southern Illinois University Press.

Bernard, Murchland, 1971, *The Age of Alienation*. New York: Random House.

Bhaktivedanta, A. C., 1968, *The Bhagavad-gita As It Is*. New York: Collier-Macmillan.

———, 1968, *Teachings of Lord Caitanya*. New York: ISKCON.

———, 1969, *Sri Isopanisad*. Boston: ISKCON.

———, 1970a, "Who Is Crazy?" in *Krsna, the Reservoir of Pleasure and Other Essays*. Boston: ISKCON.

———, 1970b, *The Nectar of Devotion*. Boston: ISKCON.

———, 1971, *Krsna: The Supreme Personality of Godhead*. Boston: ISKCON.

———, 1972a, *Srimad-Bhagavatam*, First Canto, Part One, Chapters 1–7. New York, Los Angeles: Bhaktivedanta Book Trust.

———, 1972b, *Srimad-Bhagavatam*, Second Canto, Part One, Chapters 1–6. New York, Los Angeles: Bhaktivedanta Book Trust.

Burton, Roger, and John Whiting, 1961, "The Absent Father and Cross Sex Identity," *Merrill Palmer Quarterly*, 7: 85–95.

Deloria, Vine, 1971, *Custer Died for Your Sins*. New York: Avon.

Dimock, Edward C., Jr., 1966, "Doctrine and Practice among the Vaisnavas of Bengal," in Milton Singer (ed.), *Krishna, Myths, Rites and Attitudes*. Honolulu: East-West Center Press.

Douglas, Mary, 1966, *Purity and Danger*. New York: Praeger.

Durkheim, Emile, 1956, *Suicide*, trans. by J. A. Spaulding and G. Simpson. New York: Free Press.

Eister, Allan W., 1972, "An Outline of a Structural Theory of Cults," in *Journal for the Scientific Study of Religion*, 11:319–333.

Erikson, Erik H., 1946, *Ego Development and Historical Change: The Psychological Study of the Child*, Vol. II. International Universities.

———, 1950, *Childhood and Society*. New York: Norton.

———, 1956, "The Problem of Ego Identity." *Journal of the American Psychoanalytic Association*, IV 1, p. 70.

———, 1958, *Young Man Luther*. New York: Norton.

———, 1963, *The Challenge of Youth*. New York: Anchor.

———, 1968, *Identity: Youth and Crisis*. New York: Norton.

———, 1969, *Ghandi's Truth*. New York: Norton.

Freud, Sigmund, 1936, *The Problem of Anxiety*. New York: Norton.

Fromm, Erich, 1941, *Escape from Freedom*. New York: Farrar and Rinehart.

Garfinkle, Harold, 1965, "Conditions of Successful Degradation Ceremonies." *American Journal of Sociology*, 61:420–424.

Goffman, Erving, 1959, *The Presentation of Self in Everyday Life*. New York: Anchor.
————, 1961, *Asylums*. New York: Anchor.
————, 1967a, *The Nature of Defense and Demeanor in Interaction Ritual*. New York: Anchor.
————, 1967b, *On Face Work in Interaction Ritual*. New York: Anchor.
Goodenough, Ward, 1963, *Cooperation in Change*. New York: Wiley.
Gosvami, Jiva, 1961, *Tattva-Samdarbha in History of the Vaisnava Faith and Movement in Bengal*. Calcutta: S. K. De, KL Mukhopadhyaya.
Harris, Marvin, 1971, *Culture, Man and Nature: An Introduction to General Anthropology*. New York: Crowell.
Herskovits, Melville J., 1938, *Acculturation: The Study of Culture Contact*. New York: J. J. Augustin.
Hopkins, Thomas J., 1966, "The Social Teaching of the *Bhagavata Purana*," in Milton Singer (ed.), *Krishna, Myths, Rites and Attitudes*. Honolulu: East-West Center Press.
Hoult, Thomas F., 1969, *Dictionary of Modern Sociology*. Totowa, N.J.: Littlefield, Adams.
Keniston, Kenneth, 1968, *Young Radicals*. New York: Harcourt.
————, 1971, *Youth and Dissent: The Rise of a New Opposition*. New York: Harcourt.
LaBarre, Weston, 1962, *They Shall Take Up Serpents*. Minneapolis: University of Minnesota Press.
Lofland, John, 1968, "The Youth Ghetto." *The Journal of Higher Education*, March 1968, 126–139.
Lynd, Helen, 1961, *On Shame and the Search for Identity*. New York: Science Editions.
Marcuse, Herbert, 1962, *Eros and Civilization, A Philosophical Inquiry into Freud*. New York: Random House.
Marx, Karl, and Friedrich Engels, 1939, *The German Ideology*. New York: International Publishers.
McDermott, Robert A. (ed.), 1970, *Radhakrishnan, Selected Writings on Philosophy, Religion, and Culture*. New York: Dutton.
Mead, Margaret, 1970, *Culture and Commitment, A Study of the Generation Gap*. New York: Natural History Press.
Meerloo, Joost A. M., 1956, *The Rape of the Mind*. New York: World Publishing.
Merton, Robert K., 1949, "Social Structure and Anomie" in *Social Theory and Social Structure*. New York: Free Press.
Mintz, Ira, 1973, "The Embarrassed Virgins." *Time Magazine*, July 9, 102:2.
Mooney, James, 1965, *The Ghost Dance Religion*. Chicago: University of Chicago Press.
Murphy, Frederick J., 1973, *The Pilot*. August 10.
Needleman, Jacob, 1972, *The New Religions*. New York: Pocket Books.
Parsons, Talcott, 1951, *The Social System*. New York: Free Press.
Partridge, William L., 1973, *The Hippie Ghetto: The Natural History of a Subculture*. New York: Holt, Rinehart and Winston.
Prabhavananda, Swami, and Christopher Isherwood, 1951, *Bhagavad-gita*. New York: Mentor.
Reich, Charles, 1971, *The Greening of America*. New York: Bantam.
Roszak, Theodore, 1969, *The Making of a Counter Culture*. New York: Anchor.
Sargant, William, 1957, *Battle for the Mind: A Physiology of Conversion and Brain Washing*. London: Heinemann.
Schwartz, Gary, and Don Merton, 1968, "Social Identity and Expressive Symbols: The Meaning of an Initiation Ritual." *American Anthropologist*, 70:6, 1117–1131.

Sullivan, Harry S., 1953, *The Interpersonal Theory of Psychiatry*. New York: Norton.

Tagore, Rabindranath, 1952, *Gitanjali*. London: Macmillan.

Toffler, Alvin, 1970, *Future Shock*. New York: Bantam.

Turner, Victor, 1964, "Betwixt and Between: The Liminal Period in 'Rites de Passage,'" in J. Helm (ed.), *Symposium on New Approaches to the Study of Religion*. Seattle: American Ethnological Society.

———, 1969, *The Ritual Process*. Chicago: Aldine.

Van Gennep, Arnold, 1960, *The Rites of Passage*. Chicago: University of Chicago Press.

Wallace, Anthony F. C., 1956, "Revitalization Movements." *American Anthropologist*, 58:264–281.

———, 1961, *Culture and Personality*. New York: Random House.

———, 1969, *The Trip-In Psychedelic Drugs: Proceedings of a Hahnemann Medical College and Hospital Symposium by the Department of Psychiatry*, in R. E. Hicks and P. Fink (eds.), pp. 151–156. New York: Grune & Stratton.

Warner, Wellman J., 1964, "Sects," in Julius Gould and William L. Kolb (eds.), *A Dictionary of the Social Sciences*. New York: Free Press.

Weber, Max, 1958, *The Religion of India, The Sociology of Hinduism and Buddhism*. New York: Free Press.

Worsley, Peter, 1968, *The Trumpet Shall Sound; A Study of Cargo Cults in Melanesia*. New York: Schocken Books.

Zaehner, R. C., 1960, *Hindu and Muslim Mysticism*. New York: Schocken Books.

———, 1968, *Hinduism*. New York: Oxford University Press.